The Literary Connection Volume V

My Father / My Mother = Myself

Compiled & Edited by: Cheryl Antao-Xavier

IOWI

© individual contributors, 2020

Compiled and edited by:
Cheryl Antao-Xavier

Cover image:
Shutterstock.com
(stained glass forever series)

Published by:
In Our Words Inc.
inourwords.ca
inourwords2008@gmail.com

ISBN: 978-1-989403-14-3 (paperback)
ISBN: 978-1-989403-15-0 (ebook)

The views expressed in this book are the opinions of the contributing authors. The publisher assumes no responsibility for accuracy of information or sensitivity around the issues and language used in the content.

All rights reserved. Copyright of individual stories and poems are held by the respective contributing authors and no content from this collection may be used without the permission of the respective authors. Authors may be contacted through the publisher at the above email address.

Introduction

The theme of this anthology—My Father/My Mother=Myself—drew some interesting takes on the influence of parents or guardians in shaping our lives. Some good, some bad—some fictionalized, each unique in its situation and recollection.

I thank the contributors for sharing these glimpses into their past and reflecting on their learning from the experience. There is so much to glean and understand about people from listening to their stories. Each story takes us into a fascinating world!

I hope you enjoy *The Literary Connection Volume V* as much as I did while putting it together. Enjoy the read …

Cheryl

CONTENTS

John B. Lee / 6
Darla Fisher-Odjig / 16
Honey Novick / 26
Peta-Gaye Nash / 34
elizabeth barnes / 46
Josie Di Sciascio-Andrews / 52
Kumkum Ramchandani / 62
Akemi Tomoda / 66
Michael Meik / 70
Lindsay W. Albert / 80
Norma Nicholson / 82
Bev Bachmann / 88
Harvinder Kaur Dhillon / 94
Sharon Berg / 102
Lina Alhabahbeh / 110
I.B. Iskov / 112
Gurudas Gulwadi / 116
Peter Reid / 122
Merridy Cox / 132
Lillian Khan / 136
J. Nichole Noël / 140
Miranda Wong / 144
Debra D'Souza-Haroon / 148
Susan Ksiezopolski / 152
Lynn Xu / 156
Milena Marques-Zachariah / 158
Lovina D'Souza / 162
Jasmine Jackman / 164
P.I. Kapllani / 168
Cheryl Antao-Xavier / 174

John B. Lee

John B. Lee is the Poet Laureate in Perpetuity of the City of Brantford and Poet Laureate of Norfolk County for Life. He is the author of nearly one hundred published books including *Moths That Drink the Tears of Sleeping Birds*, (Black Moss Press, 2019) and *Into a Land of Strangers* (Mosaic Press, 2019). His work has appeared internationally in over five hundred publications and he is the recipient of well over one hundred prestigious writing awards. He lives in a lake house overlooking Long Point Bay on the south coast of Lake Erie, where he works as a full-time author.

My Father's Fridge

my father's fridge
sat in the back shed
off the kitchen
there on cold cement
in the smock smells
and straw scents
of the men come in from the barn
where the collie dog slept
on the hard floor
when the winter howled at the door
by the spikes
hammered into the wall
with Ardox for hooks
and swill stink
of sour water in a galvanized pail
and apple scraps, potato peels
and the white oleogustus of rancid lard
floating in white islands
on the surface
small monocles of spoiled fat
meant for the hogs in the yard

and what he kept
in there – mostly
what my mother refused
to allow in the house

bad things
the noisome milk-rot of limburger
and blue mould
bruised in small cakes
and a sharp clabber of old cheese
and beer gone skunky in squat bottles

medicines blended
for worming the sheep
nicotine vermicides
and vials
for dosing the cattle
ewe's milk meant to be warmed
for the lambs
orphaned by mastitis
and the untimely death
of their mothers

and the damned fridge sometimes shorted
so teasing the chromium handle
in wet socks
would send an unpleasant shiver
a cruel metallic tremor
shocking the bones with a warning
noli me tangere

and now
it has all vanished
like the plowed-under autumn darkness
of a midnight field
my father working the land
in the late hours
the ghost light of his labour
dimming to nothing turning away
in the distance come close as he leaves

The Day my Mother Cut my hair

all my life till then
I'd been
an obedient boy
my hair kept short
as was my father's wish
for he believed
in a manly trim
with obvious ears
and the short-on-top
coiffeur of a farmer's son
though my cowlick
sprung at the crown
like that of a dam-groomed calf
while I feathered my collar below my cap
with the forehead tan
of working white-brained in the summer sun
for wearing my hat
with the salt-stained brim
like the coastline darkness and light
of the line of the shade at the lake
or the water-marked pages
of an old much-read book
and then
in freedom I fled
those hundred-acre men
and there beyond the scissor's reach
of my father's mind
my hair grew wild as fallow weed
one month, two months, three months
away from home in the lazy end row
of a distant school
it covered the helix, then

the cochlear swirl
then the lobes
my skull like a wilderness stone
indivisible from the green reason
a rock is born, I was born
to be loved by the open sky
like ditch-weed lace
blue chicory and all
mad grasses deep rooted
and waving their seed in the sun
and though my father
choked back rage
my mother sat me down
in a chair
washed my time-tangled hair
and gave
it shape with my sister
standing close by

and it wasn't Delilah
stealing my vigor
in the star-blind dark
of an ancient sleep
it was
my mother's hands
and her sharp surmise
in that snip and silence
with the sharp skill
of the heart
when in the red quiet
of a woman's breast
she embraces her son
and carries him forward
like the rib-shadow
of a great tree loosening its shade at gloaming

The Lonesome Postmaster of Antarctica

the year
my father
lost me to learning
was the autumn in which
he fell ill but did not die
from the fingertip of his appendix
bursting in his belly
the poison blooming
through his body
like the small shade of individual night
and he lay
in the slow delirium
of sepsis
wondering why his son
lost in that first freedom
of late youth
locked in the limestone forest
of the big city
did not write or visit or call
as from his sickbed fever
my father dreamed of himself
named in the black lists of leaning stone

and I want now all these years since then
to inform his soul
that has long since slipped
his grasp
like sleight-of-hand silk
drifting in among
the moody wood-smokes of late December

and the cold burn
of wet headlands of spring
and fogs that crawl ashore in summer
with the nimbus of every mist-gauzed moon
a monocle of sheltered light
illuminating blind rock

I did not know
though love's telepathy
should have spoken
the words I failed to hear   — *your father is ill
          almost unto death* —

but I was there
in the selfish silence
of an unquiet mind
and he was there
on the chill white landscape
of hospital sheets

a lonesome postmaster of Antarctica
in isolated darkness
listening to the whispering snows
of endless winter

John's parents: Irene and George Lee

Widowland

at the last
and
in the end
it was mostly a place
one might call
widowland
bread-warm hallways lined with
lonesome women
their men
gone to the spirit ground
and now it was a matter
of doing nothing
and no one to do it with
but a gaggle of elderly strangers
living in slow time
sleeping away
the sad-dog hours of daylight
my mother
among them
an all-girls geriatric craft class
fumbling dull scissors
in the cook smells
by the common kitchen
and she became
Lillian — a name
she never used
following the outline
the black tracing of a generic daisy
leaving a ghost
in the white page
a template for the tablecloth
green linen and coffee stain

remembering the light in cut scraps
and the sharp absence
of sliced through moments
of a lifetime
the jigsaw puzzle boxed in darkness
a chaotic configuration
no amount of shaking
will achieve the random perfection
of the night sky
shining over the apple swell
of an orchard in autumn

and there is no one
to listen to me — she says
... no one left
who has to listen to me

and it breaks the heart
to hear it
a murmur of rumours
remembering red
like the fire that follows
the bone-line
into wind-blown ashes

John's parents:
George and Irene Lee

The Visitor

now that mother
has seen two winter solstices
from the vantage
of the star-hold of the grave
with a fingernail of moonlight
trimming the lovely heavens
of a black December night
a residual lunar milk mark
set in a mostly darkening
matrilineal sky
like the lunula
of a half prayer
set in a ten-stone firmament
with beauty burned away
to a luminous crescent of haze
her soul like a wolf echo
mourning the loss of the day
an ululation of memory comes
to my sister, her daughter
remembering the summer on the Simpson farm
when the *visitor* came
and she being forever unforewarned
by what beribboned her body
a crimson lady's favour
lashing her inner thighs
and this is the life of all innocents
lost in the long lamentation
of this grown-old earth
when the primordial garden
blooms and then withers
and then blooms again
like berries in first blossom
come to crushing their hearts in the shade

Darla Fisher-Odjig

Darla Fisher-Odjig is a 7th World Aboriginal Image Maker, a fine artist and poet of First Nation lineage. Her mother Arbutus is of Dutch-French-Canadian background and her father Stanley is of the Ojibwa, Potawatomi, Odawa Nation and a WWII veteran. Her lineage has enabled the integration of Aboriginal artistry with Western/European artistry bringing a fusion and a unique vision of true Canadian fine art and poetry. Her art is part of the Indian and Inuit Art Collection at Indian and Northern Affairs Canada and she has participated in numerous exhibitions and fundraising events. Her poetry and art have been widely published including her book *My Healing Journey: A Walk in Two Worlds*.

    Darla's vision is to educate and help those who have experienced intergenerational trauma and loss. Her art and poetry is an inbred character map of the many struggles and triumphs endured through a healing journey of 22 years.

Darla Fisher-Odjig

I Am My Father

Attachment and Genocidal Ideation
(How systemic influence contributes to intergenerational trauma)

"**Genocide** is intentional action to destroy a people in whole or in part. The hybrid word "**genocide**" is a combination of the Greek word γένος ("race, people")" wikipedia.org › wiki › Genocide

As a child I have experienced in some way the systematic washing out of red blood to white blood. This story is an emotional relaying of how damaging was the enforcement of an alien cultural system on a First Nations family. The words and imaging are mine depicting the pain experienced as a child growing up in a family/community environment that had been subjected to character annihilation, cultural cleansing—as I said, white washing of red to white. My words, my projections are my own feelings experienced as best I can remember.

***

As my father returned from the hospital, I looked into his glazed, sad eyes, and saw sheer helplessness and hollowness—he was a shadow of the young person he had been. He harbours so much pain, and no one, including himself, knows what he is in need of.

It was years ago. I was a child. I could do nothing but tug on his coat. He had dark hair that swept on occasion into his eyes, and he brushed it aside in a repetitive way.

In his childhood, he was taken from his family and put into a Day School. He was puzzled as to why he could not live with his father, Dominic. He recalls running away from the school, fearful of being apprehended by the priest. He ran with a heart pounding with each step along the path to freedom. His breath was short as he tried to quieten it in the early hours of that morning of escape. Frightened as he fled for his life, he heard more pounding on that pathway, his heart and mind in a frenzy till he looked back and in relief saw that his younger brother was following him.

That day was a great escape—but only for a short while as he and his brother were caught and taken back to that Day School, that unfamiliar place, that place which for them held rejection and reform.

After the death of his mother, he and his brother were once again taken and ultimately moved off the reserve to relatives he had never known.

I can feel my father's pain as he masks that awful day as if he were talking about the weather—which I now know to be a normality for PTSD victims, a form of minimizing and coping mechanism by way of suppressing one's emotions. This sense of disconnectedness within one's own family played heavy on my father as loss of relationships and loss of self only led to a deeper sense of fight—that the goal was to survive, for death had already come.

At that time, it was common to take a child from their family and unite them with a more 'proper' or 'acceptable' parental figure. These newly-instilled ideas of family imposed a false and artificial sense of being. The children were torn away from a familiar environment and thus deprived of their authentic sense of self. These views of family unfortunately caused cultural annihilation of Indigenous peoples and was inflicted by those who regarded themselves as better and civilized, by their own standards. The result was that a false sense of guilt and shame for being unacceptable by societal norms, permeated into the unconscious cultural identity of Indigenous people.

So, there sat this young man, my father, a product of his environment. Sitting quietly with broken eyes and a diminished sense of self. He mirrored generations that fell victim to psychological genocide. They were victims of power and greed. An intrapsychic conflict of massive proportions.

My father was a warrior. All those years ago, as I looked up at him, he stood tall, his heart struggled with battle and forgiveness, a duality that tugs one way and another. In stand down mode, he watched and waited; in battle mode, he rescued and fought.

I remember my father, I remember his strengths, I remember his struggles.

I remember.

I will always remember.

Opp: The infamous Day School~ sketch by Darla Fisher-Odjig

Right: Stanley Odjig~ Darla's father

Father

(A father's love) *his fearlessness when protecting loved ones*

The dawn you kiss with your wingspread wide
As beads adorn your armoured chest
And your talons clutch for a fruitful ride
The warrior has come home to rest
Yet in the dark, his eyes they see
The dangers lurking closer still
He sets his stake to protect me
With wounded heart and teardrops fill
And in the distance angels sing
The warrior glides his wings spread wide
The beads have turned to silken wing
His talons harbour leather hide
And in his heart are feathers worn
For yet you see he is his own
The warrior lives in silence torn
And thorns upon his head he'll don.

Darla   *Stanley*   *Dominic*

Darla Fisher-Odjig

Valour Wed

(Dedication to our soldiers living and dead)

In the silence of his eyes
Drifts of smoke and battle cries
Armoured ox of endless maim
Mounds of lifeless without name
And in the corner of his eye
A touch of angel tears on high
The child is left to fend alone
Amidst the hills of silent stone
For multitudes of flowers red
A soldier true to valour wed.

(the respect of a father who carries much pain reflective of the many soldiers who died and also lived in a world much their own after the war.) I give great respect to my father.

Darla's Dad

Daddy Sweetgrass

In your eyes I see brother eagle
He watches you my sweet
In your voice I hear the loon
He rides beneath your feet
And in the distance a drum it sings
For endless songs unsung
Yours carried high by winds great wings
Awaiting feathers hung
Your chest adorned with silent beads
With leather crown secure
And moccasins that brush the seeds
Of harvests meant to cure
The beetles dance amongst your feet
A rainbow hugs the sun
And sweetgrass wisps amongst the wheat
To cushion feathers hung

My Mother

My mother met my father after the war, she was working on the Algoma Central Railway with her mother who took care of the railway work crew up in the northern part of Sault Ste. Marie. Prior to this she worked during the war in the many central areas that were set up for WWII supply stations.

My father worked on the big boats a good eight months of the year as a means of income to support the six children that would grace our family. Mom was a determined and strong woman who was very dedicated to my father and to her children. I remember her very vividly canning and preserving the many fruits and vegetables we picked and loved to eat.

Mom raised all six children. My three brothers and two sisters and myself pulled at her apron and watched as she baked her apple pies and deer roasts. She would let me help her when cooking up the rabbit that dad caught during his usual hunting treks. We all sat on the floor with many handfuls of smelts, newspaper under us and knife in hand we prepared the fish. She was not afraid to cook the wildlife brought home from the hunt and we all ate nutritional cultural foods as my mother was taught that from the bush to the pan gave us the strength we needed as growing children. We had this wonderful food given by our Creator caught by our father and cooked up by our mom.

Life was simple but fun as we were always given the choice to go off and experience life on our own. This was a special gift from our parents and we were able to learn things on our own and this made us much more confident within ourselves. My mom was very funny, but not to say she didn't endure much hardship including the loss of her first-born baby boy. In those days when a tragedy happened, the family was much alone and we certainly learned that family was the most precious gift anyone could have.

I thank my mom for all she has given us, for she taught me

that to be a woman is to be one of God's most valued gifts to man, in that she birthed, bathed, fed and played with us, nurtured and cared for us beyond her own wants and needs. To love, laugh and live, to give and share what we can, to protect and educate our children and be humbled by the greatness of our Creator.

Darla's mother ~ Arbutus

Mothers

Her rosy cheeks blushed
Like soft salmon rose petals
Carefully she brushes away
A wisp of hair
Strands of silk spun with love
The broom she holds now
She clutches with her heart
And music clouds the room
The dance has begun
Silent and gracefully she floats
Endlessly touching every inch
Of the grain filled room
She is lovely in her own way
A beauty unseen by strangers
The clouds of music lull the heart
They diminish slowly
And the music hushed
She stands alone
Clutching her broom
The day has dawned
The grain filled room still is
And she exits
Content for her heart is of gold
Shining
Rich and alive

Honey Novick

Honey Novick is a singer/songwriter/voice teacher/poet. She is a full member of the League of Canadian Poets and Poetry in Voice of the Griffin Foundation and The Writers Union of Canada. She has nine collections of poetry and eight CDs. Her most recent publication is *Undefeated Relevance*, Flowertopia Studio, 2018. Her website is honeynovick.com

My Father: the Last Milkman to Deliver Milk with a Horse and Wagon

"Did you hear about the one about the milkman's daughter?" That joke falls flat with me because I *am* the milkman's daughter and I brag about being the daughter of the last person in the City of Toronto to deliver milk with a horse and wagon, circa 1964. This is a great gift and a legacy.

Some kids would come home from school to milk and cookies. I grew up in the age of the American Bandstand TV show. The latest rock'n'roll bands and singers would play "live" and kids would dance and then rate the songs. If one was lucky enough to have a television, that kid could run home from school and be dancing at 4:00 p.m. every school day.

I did that but I also knew that if I timed it right, I could also plan to meet my father on his milk delivery route. I could then hop on the wagon, take over the reins, "click, click" my tongue in the side of my mouth and then drive back to the stables. There the horse would have the reins removed. The steel bit would be taken out of its mouth, its hide would be brushed and then sugar (placed in the palm of a hand) or an apple positioned close to the horse's mouth would be offered. After that, water in a bucket big enough for the horse to lap and quench its thirst. These were the rewards for an uncomplaining, yet easygoing companion who knew exactly where and when to stop. My father preferred giving apples because eating the apples would help exercise the horse's jaw after the bit was taken out.

I was always afraid to get too close to the horse because I thought it might kick me. It was my fear and not the horse's behaviour, even though I felt a kindred spirit with the horse who was called Teddy (or Ned, Blackie or Jimmie depending on the year they served). My father loved, genuinely loved, the horses. Only once did he have an incident where the horse tried to run away. As Lotta Dempsey wrote in *The Star*, "when a usually complacent steed decided it had been a long, hot day, headed for the cool of the stables, fortunately, Novick was in the driver's seat and was able to guide, if not slow, the breakneck speed without accident."

I had this feeling of a kindred spirit with the horses. We would look in each other's eyes and actually communicate. I know it sounds bizarre but there seemed to be a language that both my father and I had with these animals—silent or percussive or vibrational. It was a true connection, a form of education.

In 1976, Lotta Dempsey wrote about the last of the horse-drawn milkmen saying, "Milk was 11 cents a quart, and butter 25 cents a pound when Novick started working seven days a week, back in 1930. His salary? $12 a week, and for many years his delivery working hours were from midnight to 7 a.m. Then around 1944, the city passed a by-law forbidding those clop-clopping travels because the noise disturbed householders' rest. 'It's funny, though,' Novick said. 'Lots of people used to get up and come to meet me at the door at all hours. We delivered ice, too, and that was important before electrical refrigeration.'"

I actually felt a sympathetic pain when the horses were being shod. The thought of a trusting animal bending its leg and having someone take a long nail and aim it in the hole of the steel horseshoe and then using a hammer several times onto each nail four times over, pounding into the horse's hooves. Yet, the rhythm of the hooves on the cobblestones of the then streets of Toronto in the 1950s is an aural memory that lives within me to this day.

I also had nightmares when I heard about a horse being sent to the glue factory. What a metaphor! There was no way my parents could console me. I had to accept this as a fact of life even though there is a little bit of an odour/memory that lives within my nostrils.

If the horses left droppings on the road, some people who

had gardens, would come rushing out, trowel in hand, seeming to discover gold and scoop this fertile nutrient poop. Horse droppings were a valuable composting ingredient that was free for the taking (and silent gratitude given by the neighbours). One neighbour would actually figure out the times of the horse route and patiently wait until it left her a souvenir, then she would scoop it up defiantly and triumphantly add it to her garden and then when tomatoes or sunflowers were ripe, would look at the rest of the neighbours and smirk!

When I think of these vignettes or slices of a history past, I'm filled with an enrichment. I feel connected to the natural goings on of a community. Of course, times change and so did the dairy industry. The first major change was using vans or trucks to deliver milk. The most obvious and dramatic change was the large plastic bottle replacing the glass quart. Then, of course, came the ubiquitous convenient stores with milk in plastic bags. Convenient is certainly accurate. Why wait for milk delivery with the risk of a winter freezing your milk, eggs, butter, cheese when it was so accommodating to get what you need when you want it.

Several years after, horse delivery of milk, bread or ice was no longer a service allowed on city streets. My father still delivered milk with a van. He had to deal with it breaking down, a lot, especially in the cold winters. What a slog! The allure and romance of the horse pulling the wagon was gone and the harsh reality of a changing industry set in.

Of course, in time, David, my father, retired. He was always a scholar and finally had time to read and explore the city on his terms and on his own time. Yet, somehow, having a horse for a work mate was something not too many people could offer as a life history, legacy and way of knowing a different diversity.

My Father's Gift

Some men possess qualities of beauty, vulnerability,
kindness, and an ability to love unconditionally.
Knowing this was one of my father's gifts to me.

My father was a scholar who drove
the City of Toronto's last horse-drawn milk wagon.
My father loved opera, Shakespeare,
the *Talmud*, *Torah* and *Pentateuch*,
And a specially good laugh.
My father believed in freedom of speech
and encouraged me to speak up and out.
That was another one of his great gifts to me, his daughter.
Once, we saw Dr. Henry Morgenthaler driving by.
Dr Morgenthaler, the famed doctor who performed abortions
raised his fingers in the V-is-for-Victory sign.
My father said, "Why don't people leave him alone?
He's working on behalf of a woman's right to choose."
My father loved to eat. After my mother's death,
we discovered a Caribbean eatery. How extraordinary
for a Jewish man, on the Sabbath, to eat curry chicken roti,
in a palm-tree painted room while reggae music played in
the background.
For a man born in Grodno, Belarus; raised in Palestine,
ousted by quota from the USA and finally settled in Canada,
he tried to be open-minded and tolerant of all people.
Do unto others as you would have them do unto you.
If you preach something, practice it first.
That was the greatest gift my father gave unto me.

Honey with parents: David and Yocheved (Eva) Novick

My Mother the Sabra

My mother, a proud Israeli
was called a "Sabra"
"Sabra" means prickly pear, cactus fruit
An appropriate metaphor
for one thorny on the outside
numerous seeds inside and
sweet and juicy beyond imaging

I loved my mother just as I love this fruit
and found it interesting, coincidental
they are equally difficult to reach

At age eleven, my mother and I went to Israel
without my father
His work prevented him time off, he needed to earn money

after 36 years, three wars and much longing
my mother went to Israel to re-unite with her sister

This new world was an education in itself
This foreign language was spoken rapidly, gutturally
Contexts and experiences alien until
I was enticed to go picking Sabras

Method: Find tin can, unwind metal hanger,
wind then fasten hanger with a long stick onto tin can,
protect arms, legs and eyes from thorns
enter cactus grove

At first, I dithered, scared and unfocussed,
but once I determined to focus, I extended my arm,
coordinated it with can and aimed for fruit

Carefully placing apparatus onto desired fruit
I jiggled that fruit, a lot, till one after another pear
fell into can and carefully, tenderly
placed in basket, exit grove carefully

with gloved hands, pick up fruit
cut ends of thorny skin, slide knife down the middle
remove fruity pulp, bite, let juice drip down chin
fall in love, fly to heaven, devote oneself to
loving the cactus prickly pear

This was the methodology of dealing with my mother,
approach with caution, protect myself,
empathize with her needs
(this daughter of a prickly pear was becoming skilled at survival)
use guile to manipulate, focus, become stubborn,
get reward, express love, undying forever love
yet under that rough exterior was such sweetness
such goodness
just like the cactus pear reward
True love, eternally

Peta-Gaye Nash

Jamaican-born **Peta-Gaye Nash** has written six children's books and a collection of short adult fiction, *I too Hear the Drums,* IOWI, 2015. Her work appears in several anthologies. She blogs on petagayenash.com about all manner of things and teaches English as a second language to newcomers to Canada. In 2015, she won the Marty Awards for Emerging Literary Arts. Peta-Gaye is currently working on publishing her seventh children's book and her second collection of short stories for adults. She lives in Mississauga.

The Perfect Father

My father said he saw my mother at a bus stop and thought she was the most beautiful woman he'd ever seen. "I'm going to marry that girl," he said to himself.

My mother is still beautiful. A man in his seventies came up to me recently saying "Your mother is still as beautiful as ever. You know I loved her when I was a boy." Thank you, I said, wishing I'd inherited beauty like that. And my father, tall, proud, roguish, with a head of thick brown hair that still turned heads when it turned salt and pepper, then full grey, was as handsome as they came. When I look back at the yellowed wedding pictures, which no-one wants today, they look like a match made in heaven.

I am the first born: creative, curious, and perpetually in an existential crisis. Why am I here, to this family, in this country, in this time period, born to these parents? It seemed like a mistake. I needed something quite different, I thought. I wanted a soft, kind, patient, nurturing father, the kind who hugged me and told me I was beautiful. I needed a strong, no-nonsense mother who wouldn't send me to my father for help that he couldn't give.

My childhood wasn't a bad one. My parents were not unkind. But it's often those times of great distress that become our milestones and shape the people we become. Math homework will forever define who I've become. In a timid whine, I'd show my mother my math book and ask for help. Without really looking at it, she'd say, "Ask your father." I'd shrink with fear and resignation as I made my way to my parents' bedroom, walking the long hallway of darkness that separated their bedroom from mine. That hallway seemed to stretch for miles. One side was a decorative grill that looked onto a Spanish type courtyard. Beyond the courtyard was the growing darkness that seemed to envelope the house, the land around it and seeped inside the house like a vapour and surrounded my bed where I tried to do my homework.

I'd waited too long. Soon it would be bedtime and the homework still wasn't done.

I'd approach the bedroom and stand haltingly in the doorway. My father, lying in the king-sized bed with the bright blue bedspread, watched my waif-like figure standing there.

"Can you help me with my math homework?" I asked.

He was a man of few words unless he was with his friends. He nodded and I'd go over to his side and sit beside him on the bed. It didn't matter how long he explained, I just didn't get it. Stupid! I've long since let go of the hurt *stupid,* of having my book *stupid* thrown across the room *stupid,* the shouting *stupid* that I took so personally, the name *stupid* hurled at me that it felt like shards pricking every inch of my body. I carried that with me for so long and it was only until I had children that I realized what he'd battled. There were so many times I wanted to shout and scream, "what don't you understand?" So many times, I simply turned away and said, "Ask your father!" There were times when I wanted to hurl a book across a room and scream, "Don't you see that your failures are mine? Don't you see that if you don't get it, the worse will happen—homelessness, death, decay, doom?" Stupid!

We walked on eggshells around Dad, all of us, my mother and my two sisters. We tried not to arouse his anger. It could attack us at any time. I followed my mother's lead. She kept quiet. She swallowed the hurt. She never spoke up. She smiled and was positive and she called me beautiful when I was sure it was a lie. She cooked and cleaned and worked and when we moved to the United States, she indulged my love of break-dancing and hip hop music. When my father was coming home, we braced ourselves for his mood.

I asked my dad about his father. He had nothing good to say about the mild-mannered amicable man I called grandpa. "He helped everybody with their career, but he didn't help *me,* his own son. He took me to visit his friends then stayed there all day drinking and I was the ice boy. Go get us some ice."

The hurt is still there inside my dad. I think he feels his

intelligence, his penchant for remembering details, dates, wars, conversations, were wasted. He was to have been apprenticed to be a lawyer. He said his father was to have set it up but he didn't follow through. My Dad watched his friends move up, men he said were jokers or dummies in high school. Maybe he carried his bitterness into fatherhood. Or, maybe he felt like I often do: dreading the drudgery of routine and responsibility.

To everyone's surprise, my mother eventually left my father when I was a young adult. There was no screaming nor crying, no shouting or obvious conflict, just a quiet unsettling shock over everyone. She battled on alone still swallowing life's hurts. I modelled myself after her, extroverted but wanting no contention, no conflict. I swallowed all the negative things said to me and the pain it caused, the *I-should-have-saids* built up and enclosed me like a castle wall, imprisoning me into a depression. I was a victim, a waif-like adult standing there needy, wanting to avoid conflict. But it followed me.

One day, a boss I admired criticized my work unnecessarily. He was much older and towered over me in stature. I was humiliated. Something rose up inside of me, not so much like a dam that was going to break its bank and overflow, but more like an insidious trickle of water that would not be held back. Why should I let any man speak to me this way? I tolerated it for an entire childhood. Why should I let it continue? I wouldn't. I mustered up the courage, shaking on the inside, the butterflies in my stomach flitting around and batting against my stomach walls. My mouth was dry. I don't know where I found the courage. He was sitting in his chair trying to get a story out. There was a deadline. Maybe I would be a nuisance and I should turn around and go back to my desk.

"Mr. Brown," I tried not to stammer. "Please don't talk to me that way again." He looked up in shock and saw the hurt on my face. "I don't appreciate it. All you had to say was you wanted it done another way."

It was my turn to be in shock when he apologized. He never spoke to me like that again. That was a first for me and I'll never forget it.

There was the time I pulled a belligerent adult student out of my English as a second language class and told her that I was on her side, but if she continued to disrupt my class and battle me against the grammar rules *she* thought were correct, she would have to leave the class. It worked like a charm and I called my mother that night and said, "I was born in Jamaica, but I grew up in Canada. I grew up today." Then there was the time I asked for a pay raise. Or the time a family member hurt me and I spoke my mind. Each time is satisfying and I can hardly believe I'm the same person who shoved the hurt down and never said a word.

A few years ago, while I was visiting a museum in Washington D.C. the guard came up to me and asked me where I was from? I told him I was visiting from Toronto, but I was originally from Jamaica.

"I am from Guyana," he said proudly.

"Oh," I said making small talk. "We're practically neighbours."

"Ma'am," he said most outraged. "We are certainly not neighbours. Guyana is neighbour to Venezuela. Jamaica is in the Caribbean and Guyana is part of South America. We are certainly NOT neighbours."

I was in shock and indignant. "I do NOT need a geography lesson on where Jamaica and Guyana are located. I am aware that they are not technically neighbours. But you eat curry goat. We eat curry goat. Your accent sounds like mine. You eat mango. We eat mango. I was trying to be nice. You hear me. NICE!!!!!"

I left him open-mouthed. "What on earth were you saying to that man?" asked my mother, scurrying up. "I could hear from all the way over there."

"Oh, I was just trying to be nice."

And while this may seem run-of-the-mill to many, especially my friends and family members who say what they think when they think it, those tell-it-like-it-is souls no-one messes with, those stand-up-for-the-world kind of people—this is never easy for me. It always causes angst. But the more I do it, the more that little girl standing in the doorway fades. She is replaced by another little girl. This little girl flounces into her parents' bedroom and jumps on the bed. She still doesn't understand the math problems and she doesn't pretend to.

"I don't care," she says to her dad, running her hands through his thick hair. "I'll never use it anyway. By the time I'm driving, a GPS will tell me how many kilometres it is to my destination and it will calculate my arrival time. I don't care that I don't understand. But thank you for being my dad and for pushing me to stand up for myself," she says, hugging him tightly.

Peta-Gaye with her parents

It Must be a Duppy or a Gunman

Our house was said to have been built on an old Arawak burial ground and maybe when it was being built, not enough white rum was spilled on the ground to appease the spirits to stay put and not haunt the living.

The Arawaks or Tainos as they are now called, were Jamaica's aboriginals, the people Columbus found living there long before the Europeans came bringing slaves from Africa and then indentured labourers from India and China. The spilling of the white rum on construction sites was, and maybe still is a practice, to keep all the *duppies*, spirits of those people long gone, in the spiritual realm where they belonged. Belief in duppies is an accepted thing, especially for a nine-year-old child, even though adults scoffed and said there was no such thing. Proof was in the famous song that came out in 1974 *It must be a duppy or a gunman* by Ernie Smith. He was so frightened, he forgot his daughter's name so the song says. As a matter of fact, he was so frightened, he ran faster than Donald Quarry, top sprinter and gold medalist in the 1976 Olympics. That was all the proof I needed.

"I would focus more on schoolwork and less on foolishness," said my father and he muttered that there were more dangerous things to be afraid of.

"Like gunmen?" I asked.

He waved his hand dismissively at me but we soon got three Doberman Pinschers that were locked up during the day and let loose at night to patrol the yard that was fenced in by a thick, white concrete wall.

The house was built in the Spanish-style with startling white stucco walls, a red-tiled roof and a large courtyard where my mother held our birthday parties. The neighbourhood, newly built on the hill, was a move upward, away from our little bungalow in Havendale where the rooms felt small and constricted. The scheme as we called our neighbourhood, looked down on Havendale, and the road to get up and down the mountain was precarious with a cliff on one side of the narrow road that terrified me. I imagined our car would one day go careening off the side. My father drove up and down the mountain fearlessly, like a race car driver, expertly negotiating every bend, while my mother clutched the steering wheel like a life-line, peering nearsightedly over the dashboard and talking to me to distract herself from the task.

My room was separated from my parents' room by a hallway that looked down into the courtyard. A black wrought-iron grill let the outdoors in. During the day, I'd stop in the hallway and look out, holding onto the grill that spilled fresh air and sunlight on the terrazzo tile and white walls, longing to be outside and playing with my friends. But during the night, the hallway was ominous. The darkness that harboured unspeakable evils seemed to envelop the house and we were only safe inside. I wouldn't dare to touch the grill at night, lest the darkness grab my fingers and carry me through the bars to the dangers that lurked in the bougainvillea bushes and palm trees, in the trunks of the fruit trees, even growing upward from the roots of the zoysia grass that my mom had planted in our garden.

One night, after I'd been told to go to bed, I fell into an uneasy sleep. It had been a miserable evening. It was summertime and as we often did, the neighbourhood children, weary after playing in the heat, gathered in one garden to discuss the ills of the society we found ourselves in. No-one was immune from the changes in Jamaican society: the threat of communism, the rising murder rate, the empty supermarket shelves and the way no one could tell anyone else which political party their parents were voting for. One of the younger boys bragged his father had a gun. Another girl piped in. Her father had a gun too. I couldn't be outdone. My father had a gun too, I'd seen it myself, a small harmless looking black piece of iron that my father had sternly instructed me never to touch nor say a word about it to anyone. I didn't dare pick it up but one day while he slept, I crept under the bed where he kept it and placed my finger on its handle. I could feel its cold hardness on my index finger long after I'd gone back to my room.

"My father has a gun. I know where he keeps it." I must have shouted because one of the older girls shushed me with a wild fear in her eyes. She pointed to a rastaman's shack across the street.

"Dready, the rastaman can hear you. Now he knows your father has a gun. He will come in and kill all of you during the night and take your father's gun."

I wasn't only chastised, I was terrified. The end had come for my family and it was my fault. All because I'd wanted to show off. I was silent while the talk continued and was glad when we dispersed yet I was also reluctant to end the night and return home to face what I was sure would come. I walked home with a leaden chest, a churning in my stomach, like a prisoner going to his execution.

Sitting at our round mahogany table, I watched my parents eat dinner for what I thought was the last time. It was a relief to be released from the table and to finally go into bed where I could wait for the worst. I told myself that perhaps Dready didn't hear my boast and that he wouldn't come to murder my family. I swore to God that if He saved my family, I wouldn't be so stupid again. I wouldn't boast. I would be a better child and I would never again make my Barbie have sex with Ken.

Looking back, Dready was a harmless rasta whose head was encircled by a plume of smoke from the ganja he smoked daily, a man who probably had to fight to keep his home when the scheme was being built. His shack across the road was an anomaly with the high white walls of our Spanish style houses. Unfortunately, it was our house that was directly across the street from Dready's. I could hear the music he blared from my driveway and the voices of Bob Marley and the Wailers pulled me close to the concrete wall that separated our house and the road from Dready's shack. This new music confused me greatly. On one hand, you were cool if you knew the words. Some of the neighbourhood children sang along and I longed to be like them, but my father's album collection included the albums of Kenny

Rogers, Cher, and Helen Reddy. On the other hand, my grandparents' generation felt that Bob Marley's music and reggae on a whole was subversive and led down a clear path of drug use and degeneracy.

Dready sometimes smiled at me when my father drove me home from school and I got out to open the gate, but I was terrified of him and would look away. Besides, in my child's mind, I didn't know where to place that smile. Was it innocent and friendly or was Dready smiling to lure me into his shanty? I was a product of my upbringing. As ridiculous as it now seems, back then we were told that rastas were to be avoided. They were dirty, dangerous and a serious threat to society.

I awoke at some point in the night, feeling a presence beside me. I opened my eyes and saw a man lying in my bed. He lay on his back with his hand folded on his chest as in prayer. As my eyes adjusted to the darkness, I saw that his eyes were closed and he had a pleasant look on his face, almost if he was resting peacefully. I was paralyzed. I couldn't shout or the man might hurt me. I stared at him waiting for the right moment to leap out of bed. The problem was I would have to leap over the man and dash into the grilled hallway that let in the darkness. I'd have to run past the grill that looked down into the courtyard. I kept closing my eyes and opening them again, hoping that I had been dreaming, hoping that the man would disappear. The man remained motionless in my bed. After what seemed like an hour, I mustered up the courage to leap over him, running from my room down the hallway into my parents' room.

It seemed to take a long time and my legs were heavy as if I was running through water, but I kept my face forward and didn't look through the grill. I dashed to my mother's side of the bed.

"Mummy, there's a man in my bed."

She shook my father awake and they bolted from their beds. I saw my father reach under the bed for his gun. They ran down the hallway and into my room. My father turned on the light with his left hand and pointed the gun at my bed with his right. There was nothing except my green blanket, crumpled on the side where the man had lain. I couldn't believe my eyes. My father must have felt fear and relief, possibly annoyance.

One of my parents said, "It was just a bad dream," but I don't remember who. When my father left my room, I turned to my mother in bewilderment.

"I wasn't dreaming," I insisted. "I saw a man lying right there." I pointed to the space on the bed. Then my tears erupted and I confessed my 'crime.' I had betrayed my family by telling the neighbourhood my father had a gun. I thought we were going to die that night, but I had really seen a man in my bed.

My mother said my fright over Dready might have conjured up the nightmare but her face showed no sign of disbelief. The look on her face as she pulled me into her, told me she believed every word. She nodded and listened while I insisted there had been a man. It wouldn't have been unusual for a man to be in the house. Our house had already been robbed months ago while we were out. But this was different.

"I know what I saw," I said.

Long after we'd left that house and migrated to North America for a more promising future, my mother told me she had once seen a white-haired man in my bedroom in that house. She hadn't felt afraid.

"He was standing near the window staring out. He turned and looked at me and I felt a calm, peaceful feeling," she said. "And then he disappeared."

"Not enough white rum was spilled at the time of construction," I said. "The spirits on that land were restless."

We were silent as memories of that time came to life again, floating before us. There is the dangerous winding road leading to our white Spanish-style house on the hill, built on an old Arawak burial ground. There is the shack across the street, a hovel with no running water and loud reggae music spilling from its wooden walls in defiance of a colonial past. There is Dready looking down at me and smiling, his eyes watery and red. I am still puzzled by his smile. He takes a draw from a rolled marijuana joint that he calls a spliff and exhales a plume of smoke. There is the land around us, the red dirt underfoot that has to be swept from homes day after day by the help, the same land where restless spirits roam.

My mother and I take turns remembering, her voice like a song, a soft old-fashioned Calypso melody that lilts and sways before it comes to rest. Her expression is serious, contemplative and her eyes, which can be either sharp or soulful, and are as black as ackee seeds, gaze softly at something in the distance.

It is a lifetime ago and I myself am a mother now, sometimes squeezing myself uncomfortably in a single bed after my children have had nightmares. The land and that time during my childhood still come to me in dreams, and it has stirred and shaped my creative life, but it occurs to me that my mother's belief in me that night and always, gave me the courage to write the stories.

Peta-Gaye's parents' wedding

elizabeth barnes

elizabeth barnes has been writing poems for over 20 years. She has two published books—*Giving into Gravity,* IOWI, 2010 and *the way we go*, IOWI, 2019. For 20 years she worked for the City of Toronto, running fabric art and creative writing programs at a women's drop-in. Now semi-retired, she is still sewing and writing, and lives in Mississauga, Ontario.

My Mother

My mother was a walker. Whenever anything upset her, she walked. I would meet her in unexpected places, in ravines and on main roads going nowhere. I was walking too.

I never wanted to be her, but they say we inevitably become our mothers (or fathers, as the case may be). I never thought she would be like me either—soft and vulnerable, weak. I had not forgiven her. And I suspect she walked because she knew that and because she had not forgiven herself.

When we were young, she took us walking in England, all of us trailing after her like a string of ducklings over the moors and in the Lake District gathering wild hazelnuts and pushing the sheep aside.

When we were older, she'd go off on her own walk for weeks and weeks and leave us alone with father. She'd cross the Atlantic, take a train, and then begin to walk—across the moors, through towns she came upon. She'd swim in the tarns, stripped naked, and dry herself on her socks. Then she'd eat her cheese and tomato sandwich and walk on. She must have known where she was going because she always reached another B&B before nightfall. From there she walked on again the following morning. Like some demented minstrel with no song to sing.

Then she'd come home, all walked out, ready she said, to resume the burden of her family.

I never wanted to be like her, but she taught us to walk, to swing our legs from the hips. Said she'd make walkers out of us, she would. For that I was thankful.

My mother the walker.

We lived one summer at Ravenscar on the east coast of Yorkshire, in a big, dark house set high on a clifftop. There was the black dog, Fiona, who came with us to the beach, to the cave and into the cold North Sea. There were cats that ate mother's pies as they cooled on outside window sills. We walked up and down the steep inclines along the cliffs to Robin Hood's Bay and beyond to Whitby. We searched for fossils and jet on the beach and in the shops.

My mother the rock hound.

She taught me to love geology and minerals, to love the sky and the weather it brought, the trees, the birds, the water—all the natural things of this world. So much so that when there was no mother to turn to, I turned to the forests and the thunderstorms, the moose at the edge of the lake.

I learned to run barefoot from May to September, the cool ground damp beneath my feet.

I learned to pick wild strawberries, blueberries, and raspberries, the brambles drawing blood on my arms. The sun on my shoulders. The insects buzzing in the hot air. Memories of summer.

She taught me the elementary backstroke in the cold Atlantic waters off the coast of Scotland.

My mother the nature-lover.

My mother taught me the meaning and affect of being passive-aggressive. She taught me how to do it to another when she shut me out for hours, for days, because I had annoyed her. The grand old silent treatment.

My mother the passive-aggressor.

She taught me to knit and sew.

I learned to love food and the subtleties of food preparation from my mother.

She taught me to work hard and do everything myself like a pioneer, from dawn to dusk.

My mother the home-economics teacher.

I didn't want to admit that I learned all this from my mother because I hadn't forgiven her. For what? For not loving me enough? For being above all efficient and lacking empathy? I'm not sure.

My mother taught me much. She taught me to be independent, to take care of myself, never to ask for help and not to talk about myself. I learned not to care too much, not to commit but to stand back and pass judgement, to watch myself, be wary, not to give myself away. But then I did. Give myself away.

She could be hard and cold and all business. But she got old and soft, forgot how to do things, forgot we were her children.

Do mothers teach their daughters so much these days? And what do they teach their sons?

elizabeth's parents taken in 1969

Shifting Paradigm

In a cloud of bubbling cranberries,
steaming rice and left-over chicken bits,
crisp & vinegary pickles yield to my knife
and the ghost of my mother
appears before me.

I shift, unbalanced,
and for once in my life,
I long for her to be
by my side, talking to
me, engaged in my life,
wanting desperately to know
me, and I, wanting to know
what drove her, and held her
firm—to know what force
called her to the basement
where, night after night,
she slouched, a hunched wild-haired silhouette,
over fizzing chemical droplets,
light-refracting microscopes, and
tiny numbered samples of glittering bits—
quartz, mica, feldspar, tourmaline, raw opal,
and other not-yet-identified shards and shapes
unearthed from the Dundas quarry and
the outback of Australia.

Photo credit: Lindsay W. Albert

Josie Di Sciascio-Andrews

Josie Di Sciascio-Andrews is a poet, author, teacher and the host & coordinator of the Oakville Literary Cafe Series. She has authored six poetry collections, the most recent being Sunrise Over Lake Ontario, 2019. She has two nonfiction books. Josie's poetry has won two literary prizes and has been shortlisted for several others. Josie teaches workshops for the Griffin Award's Poetry in Voice and Oakville Galleries. She writes and lives in Oakville, Ontario.

"Walking, I am listening to a deeper way. Suddenly all my ancestors are behind me. Be still, they say. Watch and listen. You are the result of the love of thousands." Linda Hoga, 1947. (Native American Writer)

My parents story

My father met my mother in 1954, in the decade after the end of the Second World War, a conflict for which he had not been a soldier because he was too young to be drafted. A war which had nonetheless, left indelible scars of trauma and poverty in the heart and landscape of post-war Italy. He was twenty-five and worked for ACEA, a post-war national electrical company, precursor of what was to become ENEL.

Having to stop his high school studies in Lanciano because the Nazis had bombed the railway tracks, my father decided to alternately get a diploma as an electrician from his hometown's *liceo tecnico*. With this, he was soon hired by ACEA to install wiring along the roadways of communities throughout the country. It was a project funded by the Italian government in its aim to rebuild and modernize the infrastructure after the disastrous devastation of World War II, in those Fifties of golden promise and technological progress. ACEA stationed trucks of workers all over Italy, in various areas in need of electrical power. My father's crew was sent to Macerata, a province of Le Marche, several hours away from his home region of Abruzzo.

On one particular morning, while they were installing hydro wires, along the unpaved gravel roads of the tiny village Cessapalombo, my father met my zio Nino, who was riding home from work on his Vespa. Had they never met, I wouldn't be here to write this story, because it was the spark of that instantaneous friendship that led to his finding my mother. After striking up a conversation with my father, my uncle had invited him and the other workers to drink some fresh water from the outdoor well in the garden of his house. Thirsty and feverishly sunburned in the scorching summer sun, the men had eagerly accepted the kind offer. The invitation was opened up for them to return for cool water any time they needed. It was on one of those thirst-quenching refreshment pauses that my father saw my mother for the first time, and in a cliché *coup de foudre,* instantly fell in love with her.

She was sitting on a bench, sewing in the shade of a hazelnut tree, tacitly absorbed by her task. She was eighteen, had only been home a year from a three-year college residence in a cloistered convent run by nuns, where her mother had placed her to learn the fine art of embroidery. My mother had not liked her stay there and I used to ask her often, why she had never complained or begged not to go, to which she always replied that she couldn't complain because after the war, times were tough and often there wasn't enough to eat. Going to school at the monastery was a good way of getting a free education and sewing skills to make a living. But three years in a cloistered monastery were difficult, although peppered with the unavoidable beauty of friendships, budding aspirations and youthful enthusiasm that can only bloom once in the life of a young person between the ages of fourteen and seventeen.

The nights the girls spent whispering in their dormitories under the nuns' threats to be quiet and to go to sleep or not be fed breakfast the following day; the not being fed the next day regardless of how loud they had been; at noon, watching mother superior at the head table indulging on giant turkey drumsticks, mounds of potatoes and dessert, while the rest of the girls faced a glass of water and a plate with one piece of stale bread and cheese. Thank God for the apple tree in the courtyard! The girls could eat all the apples they wanted from what they

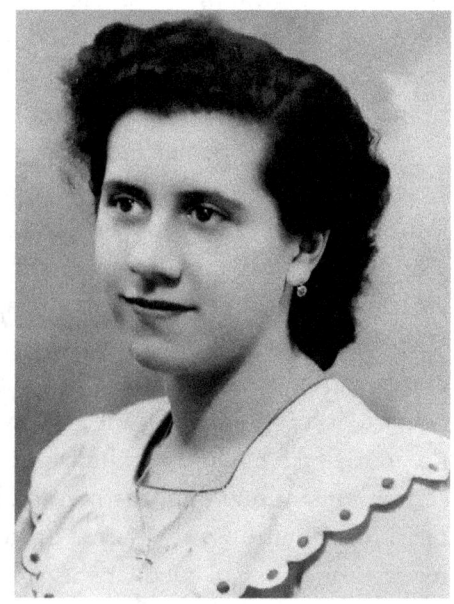

Josie's Mum: Iolanda Paoletti, circa 1952

could reach up to pick or what fell on the cobblestones. I used to ask her why she didn't beg her mom to take her home, on those days she came to visit. My mother said she had thought of it. In fact, it was the only thing she wanted more than anything. She had even written letters several times and hid them in her sweater, to sneak them to her mother through the small metal grate opening in the bolted portal, but never summoned the courage to follow through with it, for fear of disappointing everyone. It was only in those brief moments that she could talk to her mother, touch her face and exchange gifts, which she brought for my mom each time: baskets of snacks and clothes, a new red coat one year at Christmas, the colour of which the nuns frowned upon, as it was too extravagant for a young woman in whom they were trying to instill the values of restraint and humility. Austerity, sacrifice, simplicity and discipline: these were the qualities introduced to my young mother's psyche, to which, out of goodness of character, already primed in childhood by the deprivations of war, she obliged and excelled. In a graduation letter from

Josie with her Mum

her teacher, she shone as one of their top students in ability, skill and comportment. She was indeed, beautiful! Milk white skin and raven curls. Her brown eyes, her sweet gentleness must have thunderstruck my father on the fatidical day his gaze unwittingly fell upon her. Entranced by the spell of her momentary, momentous vision, when sweltering hot and exhausted, to quell his thirst, he heartily retrieved the rope and pitcher of icy water from the well.

Josie with her mother

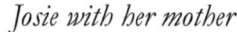

For days and weeks this continued, with my mother unaware. My zio Nino, who was now on best friends terms with my father and all the other men from the hydro company, was coaxed by him to be introduced to his younger sister. So it was soon after, that zio Nino started inviting my father to the house for meals. To my mother, who was only eighteen, he at twenty-five, must have seemed a lot older and she had made it clear that she was not remotely interested. Infatuated instead, my father did not relent in his attempts to gain my mom's esteem. So, even when ACEA's work was completed and the young electricians packed up for Abruzzo, my father returned often, either alone or with a friend, to visit zio Nino, my mother and her whole family, who by now, were all enamoured with my dad's amiable personality, his wit, humour, intelligence and generosity. From one such trip to see my mother, we have a black and white photograph. My father, dapper in his tweed coat and she, lovely in her red one, both young and smiling, standing by his motorcycle.

The back-story they used to both tell me was that right before Christmas of 1954, all dressed up and handsome, my father had arrived on his motorcycle to claim my mother as his bride. He had inserted newspapers under his coat to protect his chest from the cold wind, as he rode five hours along *l'Adriatica* from Casoli to Cessapalombo, the only route in the fifties, before the *superstrada* was built decades later. When he arrived, he unwrapped boxes and boxes of gifts strapped to the back of his motorbike: a huge one with a beautifully frosted confection his mother had especially baked for my mother. It was sponge-cake imbued with espresso and rum, in layers filled with three types of cream pudding, butter sugar frosting on top and tiny silver candy beads spelling the words: *amore* and *Iole,* my mother's name. This and many other boxes with clothes, a gold watch, earrings and, in the last little blue one, a diamond ring. My mom must have been moonstruck, not just by the gifts, but by my father's good looks and charm. My father at twenty-five, with his green eyes and fair, slicked back, curly hair; his winsome, handsome face; his charismatic voice as he told her stories of his adventures in the service or travelling through Italy. She was overtaken by him and his kindness. She accepted the ring, much to the joy and approval of her sisters, brother and parents, who were eager to make my dad part of their family. In the words of my mom's father, who had fought in World War I, was a great judge of character and who by now adored my father, my mother was lucky to marry *un gran brav'uomo (a great young man)*.

It was the Christmas of 1954 and as it was customary in Italy in those days, young people did not date. So as soon as my mother accepted my father's marriage proposal, a small wedding celebration was planned for right after *Natale,* on New Year's Day of 1955. This was also because my father lived so far away, money was scarce and it was expensive to travel back and forth. They married right after the holidays, in winter, in a small chapel of a monastery in Colfano, presided by a monk, with family and close friends in attendance. It was both a joyous and sad event in

Josie with her parents:

Iolanda and Luigi Di Sciascio

my mother's tender life, that only in retrospect I now fully comprehend. It was with mixed feelings, the kind that come with all kairos moments in one's life, that she embraced my father, love and the future, by opening her arms to her new married life in a far away town and said goodbye once again to her beloved family and Le Marche. The promise my father gave to keep her was a house of love and happiness, a wedding reception in his hometown and a honeymoon. For the most part he kept his promise. As young as he was, he had rented a two storey house with a balcony on each floor, in the historical quarter of Casoli. It was replete with top of the line, new furniture and appliances. As it was customary in those days in Italy, his mother had set it all up with bridal *corredo* or fine linens, silverware and china. Papa' had also chartered a black FIAT *Berlina*, to drive them to the church ceremony in Casoli and to the wedding reception at his parents' homestead in Piano dei Mulini.

We have only one black and white photo of my parents at their wedding, and it's a bit blurred. My mother and father are sitting by each other, holding hands and happy. There are family members and friends all seated beside them. Behind them is a window with light shining in. A garland of greenery and roses adorns the white muslin cloth of their wedding table. Porcelain plates filled with delicacies catered by my grandmother and crystal glasses filled with my grandfather's home made wine. In our family photo albums this picture was one of my favourites. There are others too, of my mother and father near the well after their engagement, and of them standing together by the *portone* of my mother's parents' house. There's a photo of the FIAT *Berlina* and of my dad's father in his fedora. One of nonna standing by the gate, under the grape trellis, and one of my mother sitting in a field of daisies and one where, newly married, in a white blouse and polka-dotted skirt, she's sitting beside a beautiful German Shepherd on the stone steps of Casoli. Old photographs of my father too, dispatching radio messages in his army uniform, headphones and a moustache, during his eighteen month stint in Tuscany, during Italy's mandatory army program *a fare il soldato*. Then pictures of me as a baby. My beautiful, young mother holding me. So many photographs after that. *Mamma* on the balcony with her sister and friends carrying me. *Mamma* and *papà* smiling at each other on nonna's terrace, with me standing in front of them. Me in *zia Enrica's* arms. Me with *nonna* and *nonno*. Years, decades of photographs of us, and then my younger sister's wondrous addition to the family. Her baby pictures, and then all of us in so many photo albums now stacked in my mother's living room.

There was so much more to happen beyond those moments frozen in stills. So many additions, changes, erasures. So many more stories to be told, yet today I wanted to write about how two young people's lives haphazardly came together to procreate my own life. So much beauty they shared! So much love! So much well meaning positivity! So much history in both of their incarnations! It would take volumes to unravel the sacredness of their lives' code and lineage. They gave me the universe. Treasure from the flames of two lit candles. For so long now their light has gone out, but continues in my sister, in me and in my children's being. My father's love of music. His love of words and books. His intelligence, his kindness, love of friends, of travel and history. His generosity and love of all wondrous things. My mother's gentle beauty, her talent and preciseness in her embroidery, sewing and everything she touched. Her humility, kindness and compassion. Her strength of character. Her miraculous ability to bring peace, comfort, happiness, beauty and order to any situation. Her love of cooking and flowers. Her story telling ability. I will never live up to their perfection. Although I write all this out of love to preserve their memory, my words pale in their shimmering shadow. They are the authors of me, of my skill, of my success, if any. I cannot ever let them down, so I extend my mind, my heart and hand, holding this pen to paper, this morning that I am here writing all this, because they lived and loved, strived and hoped, each to fulfill a dream. I am despite all differences and failings, their hope, their blood and sum. All their traits intertwined in my flesh and personality. I am my father's and my mother's extension through space in this segment of time I call my living years. My parents: children of the war. Children of an emerging, idealistic Italy trying to unite. Children from two disparate regions, two disparate cultures: Le Marche's medieval Vatican State and Abruzzo, combining the peace loving strength of the Samnites and the Franco-Bourbon values of the Kingdom of Naples. A conglomerate of history, dazzling landscapes, musical, artistic, intellectual and spiritual essences. I am that: *una piccola Italia* away from its motherland body.

My hand as it writes, reaches back to hold my parents' hands, to caress their benevolent faces and their cherished hills of olives and cypress in Casoli and Cessapalombo. Dark swallows are flying in and out of church bell towers, gliding down through blue to the sunlit valleys and the salty seas. Along the roadways, the hydro wires my father stitched along the skyline still stand. Seamed like silk from my mother's thread and needle along the cloth in her embroidery hoop, these words I weave into this story are my own life, a tapestry, a book of DNA blooming, my light braided from their light, their world and their love.

Josie's parents: Iolanda Paoletti, circa 1952
Luigi Di Sciascio, circa 1949

Kumkum Ramchandani

Kumkum Ramchandani strongly believes that our adult personalities are shaped by our childhood influences. "After that it is up to us to determine how we want to go," she says. She is a published author and poet and an artist with several exhibitions of her mosaics, handpainted stoles and paintings under her belt. She has lived in India, Africa, the Middle East and Canada and claims that she is a restless wanderer.

My Father, My Father

I cannot remember a single time in my childhood or adult years when my father kissed me or even hugged me. In the sixties, in my youth, no-one questioned family relationships. It was what it was.

I do know that I am not a demonstrative person, in fact I respect my personal space too much, and fervent hugging makes me uncomfortable. I also find it very hard to say "I love you."

My father was always a remote figure when we (my older brother and I) were growing up. He was an officer in the Indian Air Force. Every morning, after endless cups of tea and numerous cigarettes, he would put on his khaki uniform and clip on his medals. His dark blue cap would make him look dashing. He would gather up his briefcase and for about eight hours would disappear into a remote world about which I had no inkling.

I was not interested in knowing what he did or where he went. All I know is that even the walls of the house seemed to heave a sigh of relief when he left. My mother, plagued by a nervous disposition, often took to her bed with a migraine. My brother, four years older than me, would bully me mercilessly and I would wail ceaselessly, feeling free to let loose.

I became aware that my father did not behave like a lot of other fathers. I had started going to friends' homes for birthday parties and occasional sleepovers. I saw some of my friends' dads who were jovial and friendly, and hugged and kissed them.

One day my parents and I were walking in a park. We had a dog and my dad had let him loose and was carrying his metal chain link leash. A small ragged boy was following us and in a whiny voice trying to sell us peanuts. My dad told him to go but the boy persisted. In a fit of rage my dad hit him with the dog chain. The boy began to bleed from a gash on his head and his wails could be heard across the garden. Soon an angry crowd gathered around. Unsavoury people began to threaten my dad. My mum and I were crying by this time. My dad was told to take the boy to the hospital. We bundled him into the car and took him to the Air Force clinic where he got several stitches.

Even today I shudder to think of this incident. I can taste the fear at hearing my mother's pitiful cries…

My father's temper became worse day by day. Or maybe I was just becoming more aware of things as my child's protective cocoon began to wither away. My father would rant at the house help. They had to tiptoe around the house silently. If they made a racket washing dishes or arguing with each other, my father would charge at them roaring like a bull and threatening them. More often than not, they would quit, adding to my mother's burden.

My father was a foodie. Every meal in our house had to be perfect. My mother spent the major part of her day preparing for these meals and prepping with the cook. Dinner was at sharp eight-thirty and we had to be at the table or else.

Dinner would consist of very interesting dishes, not always Indian. Having served in the British Royal Air Force during the Second World War, my dad had inherited a taste for Western dishes. We would have tomato and leek soup or toad-in-the-hole or Viennese cutlets, mashed potatoes and gravy or shepherds pie. We had a different pudding every night, things like caramel custard, gooseberry tart, home made ice cream or rhubarb with thick cream.

If the dinner was late in coming, improperly served or too hot or too cold, my father would throw a fit. Instead of enjoying the array of interesting dishes in front of us, we would very often be shivering in nervous anticipation, waiting for the sparks to fly, making the food turn to ashes in our mouths.

When I was in my late teens, I began to smoke and drink alcohol. Everything illicit I did made me feel guilty. I even went on a few dates with the help of my friends who vouched for me saying that I was spending the night at their place.

Strangely, my father had no problems with my smoking or drinking but he was very adamant that no boys should enter his house. By now I was in college so it was quite easy to meet members of the opposite sex away from home.

However, because of my father's strange aversion to my having boy friends, I, for a long time, developed a sense of guilt about my interest in the opposite sex. I felt I was doing "something dirty" (his words) by having sexual feelings. It took me a long time to get over this guilt and realize that I was normal.

When I met my future husband, and made my intentions about marrying him clear, my father, for the first time in my life, struck me and locked me in my room. He couldn't bear the thought of my having made such a momentous decision on my own. However, given that I was over twenty-one and able to have a court marriage, he had to relent eventually.

My father retired early, at the age of fifty. By this time, I was married and had left India to live abroad. When I visited him with my husband and two kids, I realized that he had mellowed. He seemed to enjoy his retirement, pottering around in the garden and going out for errands to the bank or post office.

I never really sat down with my dad and talked over things because I told myself I was too busy with my job and raising my two daughters. I always made excuses not to bring up uncomfortable topics. In retrospect, I feel that I should have plucked up enough courage and maybe we would have started a new relationship on a different footing.

My father died of a heart attack when he was 73. I was not in the country and I was told that he didn't suffer much. By this time, I had learned from some close relatives that my dad had had a very sad childhood. He lost his birth mother at the age of five. His father remarried and his stepmother was very mean to him. My dad was a quiet and sensitive child and after the birth of his stepsisters and stepbrother, he became even more withdrawn.

Today, I understand my father's nature in the light of his emotionally deprived childhood. I cannot forget the anguish he put me through, but I have forgiven him. We are all creatures of our circumstances. Some of us manage to transform ourselves, some cannot.

Rest in peace, dearest dad…

Akemi Tomoda

Akemi Tomoda came to Canada in 1970 from her native Japan, following her marriage to husband Ken. She did not speak English at the time. In the years since, she has studied English and art, particularly watercolour painting. She is a devout Christian and regularly journals her 'testimony' of God's blessings in her life. She published *Akemi's Journal*, IOWI, 2011, which has been translated into Japanese. She continued to write as a form of healing and gratitude and published *Akemi's Journal 2*, DL/IOWI, 2017. She lives in Mississauga, where she is busy with her favourite hobbies of gardening, sewing and Bible study.

My Father, My Mother and Me

My father, Minoru Tanabe, was born in a rice farm in a little village in Hiroshima prefecture. He was the second last child of ten siblings. When he finished high school, he wanted to study more, but his family did not have much money. My father asked his eldest sister who was married to a rich farmer to support him and so he continued to study at a teacher's collage in Hiroshima. He became a teacher and later became a principal.

My father was a very gentle, kind and patient person. He enjoyed reading books, playing table tennis and gardening. He had quite a big vegetable garden beside the house and supplied all the vegetables we ate. He also planted a fig tree at the edge of the vegetable garden. The fig tree grew so big and started bearing fruit. My brother George, my sister Sanae and I picked ripe figs from the tree and enjoyed eating them in the garden. They were so sweet and fresh. They were so good!

While I was attending an elementary school, my father was the principal of the school. We had a gathering every morning at the school yard and every student from grade one to six lined up, and the teachers stood in front of the students facing us and my father stood on the wooden stand and gave the students words of encouragement. I enjoyed listening to my father. After he retired, he became a gardener and truly enjoyed gardening.

My mother, Midori, was born in a Shinto priest's house on a little island. She was also second last child among ten siblings. When she was in grade 5, her mother died. At that time, her elder sister was already married and wasn't at home, so my mother started looking after the family, cooking, cleaning etc.

One day after school my mother visited one of the school teachers and asked her to teach her how to sew kimonos and so the teacher taught her. Since then my mother started sewing kimonos for her father, brothers and a young sister.

She was a good seamstress. I did not know how she

learned, but she was able to make my blouse and skirt from her kimono. During World War II, we did not have anything, so that my mother made all my clothes. She was also an excellent cook. My father often invited school teachers to our home and my mother cooked all the meals so wonderfully.

She raised three children and helped with the gardening. For several years she was a leader of the village women's group and attended meetings and went on trips with the ladies.

After my father passed away, she started enjoying art, Japanese painting, origami and flower arrangements.

My parents went through very hard times during World War II, but they tried their best all the time and they both passed away very peacefully.

Now I have become a Christian and am living in Canada, so I have a different lifestyle from my parents, but I inherited so many things from them.

I enjoy gardening like my father did. I feel so comfortable when I am in a garden just like I am at home. I also enjoy sewing. Since I live in Canada, its very difficult to find my size of clothes, so I make my own clothes except for jackets. I still enjoy doing that. Unfortunately, I did not inherit a gift of cooking. My sister Sanae got that.

I also got an artistic gift from my mother. My grandfather was a very good Japanese painter, so I received this artistic gift from my mother's side of the family. I enjoy watercolour painting so much! After losing my husband, time spent painting has helped me and comforted me a lot.

I am very thankful for the gift I received from my parents. I can do gardening, sewing, painting with such joy and they make my life meaningful.

I still love to eat figs. I buy fresh figs in the summer and dried figs in the winter and enjoy eating them, remembering the time I enjoyed eating figs with my brother and sister from the tree my father had planted.

Akemi inherited her grandfather's and mother's artistic talent and her father's love of gardening. Her painting of her garden is on the cover of her book Akemi's Journal 2 (below) and several are inside the book.

Michael Meik

Michael Meik was born in Peshawar, Pakistan in 1963 to Harold and Grace Meik. The nomadic lifestyle of an Air Force family gave him a sense of adventure and numerous thrilling and traumatic memories, all of which were recounted in highly entertaining detail by his beloved parents who have both passed on. He was inspired to write his family memoir, which includes the two excerpts given below, for the benefit of the next generation.

He says "This is dedicated to you, Skylar, Morgan and Tyler."

My Mother, My Inspiration

January 2, 1929, a North Western Railway train leaves Kundian Station in Punjab, India, the guard on the train Edward and his wife Dorothy are travelling to the Holy Family Hospital in Rawalpindi for the delivery of their baby. They are alone in the caboose when Dorothy suddenly goes into labour. The baby can't wait, and Edward has no choice, but to deliver his daughter. Grace Elizabeth Mable Waterfield is born, she is my mother, the epitome of the term "Railway Children." She was referred to as Gem.

Gem's happiest memories were in Kundian. Her mother had the healing touch and she cared for any injured, sick and abandoned animals that she found. People brought their pets to her as well and there was always a menagerie of dogs, cats, ducks, geese, and even a deer, donkey and mongoose. Gem learnt to have empathy for animals as well as people at an early age. And many years later, following in her footsteps, I volunteered with Lady Constantine at the SPCA, handing out medication to owners of sick working animals in the carriage stands [ed. *horse-driven carriages*] in the poorest communities of Karachi.

My love of singing and acting also came from Mom, not forgetting the mischievous streak we both had. She had a beautiful voice, joined the school choir, plus landed the part of Robin Hood which they enacted at nearby forests. Area dignitaries and soldiers of Scottish regiments stationed in Murree would attend. On Sundays the troops sat on the lower level in the chapel, while the girls sat in the balconies, pelting peas at the soldiers' heads from above and even releasing cicada bugs on occasion, which spun noisily down the aisle. They were expected to put at least two annas into the offertory plate, but instead objects like metal buttons were dropped in the bag and their two annas were saved for old Charley's weekly visits with his steel trunk filled with all kind of sweets and candies. I was always up to mischief myself while in school, though I rarely got caught, and boy, do I have a sweet tooth!

In 1945, Gem's mother took seriously ill, and at just sixteen, she was taken out of school to care for her. They lived in Sibi, Baluchistan at the time, one of the hottest places on earth, and as such was used by the British Army as a 'punishment station.' A year later her mother passed away.

It was here in Sibi that Gem met my Dad, Harold. I have never tired of hearing this story of how my parents met, how she disliked him at first, as he teased her and treated her like a little girl. Although, she thought he was quite handsome. Dad's attempts to get past her father to meet her were hilarious and in vain.

Harold was five years older than Gem and already with the R.A.F. Police during WWII, and he was stationed all across India, Burma and Ceylon. With Partition imminent, the R.A.F. left India in March 1947, so he transitioned over to the Royal Indian Air Force. On August 14th the same year, Partition was declared, and Dad opted for Pakistan as his parents were settled in Karachi.

My Mom had completed her nurses training and joined the Army Nursing Core as a Lieutenant in the Pakistan Army, working at the Combined Military Hospital there.

At the time, women in the armed forces were not allowed to marry, and in military circles Mom going out with Dad was frowned upon, as she was a Lieutenant in the Pakistan Army and he was only a Flight Sargent in the Royal Pakistan Air Force. In 1954, they took time off together, and went to his parents' home in Lahore, secretly got married on November 27th with a few close friends and family present. The wedding was a funny event, Mom's father was unable to be there, so she was given away by Dad's stepfather. Having a flat tire on his motorbike, Dad rode to Church on his mother's ladies' bicycle, losing the wedding ring in the bargain, and when the time came to exchange their vows, he couldn't find it, so his mother took off her own wedding band for Dad to put on Mom's finger. Their reception was held in the home where the movie *Bhowani Junction* was later filmed in 1956, owned by a family friend Mrs. Holmes, who prepared all the food and even made their wedding cake.

My parents had three children, Linda, Vivian and me. On January 1973, I was nine, when Linda suffered a massive heart attack. Clinging to Dad she pleaded with him, "Daddy, I know this time I'm going to die, please save me, I don't want to die," as she went into cardiac arrest. He revived her twice before the ambulance arrived, but her heart stopped a final time in the hospital, and they could not bring her back. Mom was at work, and never forgave herself, as Linda's words rang in her ears constantly "Mummy, if I ever have one of my bad attacks when you're at work, I will die." Mom never worked again, and Dad took early retirement.

Dad had pulmonary fibrosis and died in my arms on Linda's death anniversary in 2010. Mom took it badly, ending up in hospital for a month. She passed away from cancer in November 2016. I sat with her every night till the early hours for her final three months. Her mind was good to the end, we talked, worked on the family tree and did crosswords together. She was my mentor, my friend and confidante.

I never got tired of Mom's stories of her childhood and us as kids. I celebrate my parents lives by writing their memoirs, this is just an excerpt from the full family story still to come.

Michael's Mum Grace Waterfield, with her mother, 1939 and portrait, 1952

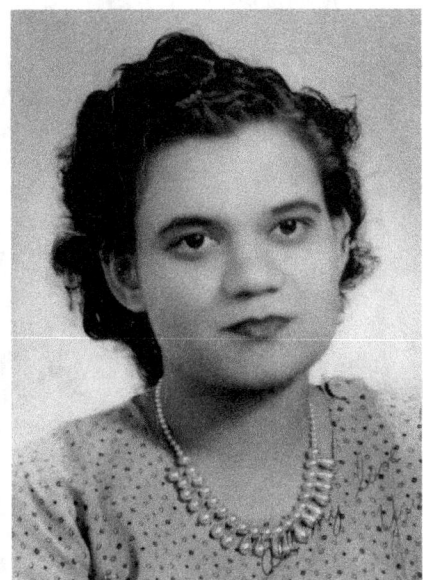

Top left:
Grace Waterfield
Pakistan Army
Lieutenant, 1951

Top right:
Harold Meik
Royal Pakistan Air
Force Police, 1950

Above:
Michael and his Mom in
1963

Left: Michael (right)
with his Mom, sister and
brother, 1972

My Father, My Hero

On September 28, 1924, my dad Harold was born to Lorenzo and Maud Meik in the small town of Baj Baj, situated on the banks of the Hooghly River in India. Lorenzo, a chartered accountant, was the controller for the Burma Oil Company, and Maud was an opera singer who performed regularly in the Throne Room at Government House in Calcutta.

Harold had a privileged upbringing until age five, which is when Lorenzo started to drink, eventually losing his job after showing up drunk to work. He would disappear for days, leaving Maud alone with Harold. In serious debt, they soon lost the house, so Maud took him to live with her parents Eugene and Elizabeth Marshall, who ran a chummery for bachelors working for the North Western Railway in Karachi.

Harold started school at St. Patrick's, and later went to St. Fidelis' in Mussoorie, India, which was run by Irish Patrician Brothers. He befriended an Anglo-Burmese boy Seaton; both were regularly singled out and caned for the slightest thing by one particular Brother. The beating got more severe, having the boys drop their pants, stand cheek to cheek, then separating them with a swipe of his cane, drawing blood on several occasions. One day during a caning Seaton snapped, knocking the man to his knees, he grabbed a knife

Right:
Harold Meik
with his mother Maud

from the table and held it to his throat, "you sick son of a bitch, if you ever lay a hand on Harold or myself again, I'll slit you from ear to ear." Shaking with fear, he collapsed on the floor in tears, he knew he had gone too far this time. Deciding to run away that night, the boys put a few things in pillowcases, snuck out before breakfast, hitching a ride on a horse cart to the railway station. The little money they had saved up, was only enough to get them to Bombay.

Noticing two young lads travelling alone, a poor Hindu farmer and his family looked out for them throughout the journey, giving them food and blankets until they got to Bombay. When disembarking, the wife gave them a blessing and told them to look out for each other. Having no money, they slept on park benches, stealing fruit off trees to survive, they earned a few rupees doing menial labour for merchants. Then one day they saw a poster, the British Navy was recruiting, but you had to be at least eighteen to apply. Both being quite tall, they bluffed their ages and went off to the recruiting office, passing a full physical and cognitive exam with flying colours. They were assigned to a minesweeper that was

Below left: With Seaton (middle) and friend, 1941
Right: Royal Indian Air Force Police, March 1946

anchored near the Gateway of India.

The Captain told them their ship, a mine sweeper, patrolled the bay and had laid submarine nets to prevent German and Japanese subs from entering the river systems. Assigned cleaning duties, their Navy careers were short lived, as the Captain treated them like dirt, referring to Harold as a Black Bastard. While mopping the engine room one day, he purposely kicked over their pales of dirty water, telling them to clean it up. Harold punched him instead. Seaton hit him again, and losing his balance, he fell over the railing into the engine bay below, severing his arm. The mechanics who hated the Captain just as much, said the boys never touched him, he tripped and lost his balance. The investigation came up empty, their actual ages were discovered, both were thrown out of the Navy, and the Captain returned to England.

It was now 1943 and WWII was in full swing. The boys decided to part ways, Seaton joined the Merchant Marines, Harold enlisted in the R.A.F., was sent to Radar School in Calcutta, and then to a Canadian-operated secret Radar Base in Panagar. Finding the pace too slow, he applied to the R.A.F. Police School in Simla. On completion, he joined the Special Investigations Branch in Delhi where he was sent on cases across India, Burma and Ceylon. By 1946 he had opened several Provost Units across the subcontinent. That year he witnessed the worst of humanity during the horrendous sectarian violence in Calcutta, nearly ten thousand Hindus, Muslims and Sikhs lost their lives. Bodies were piled high and to prevent the spread of disease, they loaded them into military trucks and set them ablaze.

By March of 1947, the R.A.F. returned to England and Harold transitioned over to the R.I.A.F. Then on August 14th, Partition was declared; Pakistan was born, causing the displacement of over 15 million people, nearly two million lost their lives, friends killing each other in ways too horrific to describe.

As Harold's parents had settled in Karachi by now, he opted for Pakistan. He got orders to move a convoy of trucks filled with rare books from a Muslim library in India to Lahore. Driving through Amritsar, they passed thousands of slaughtered men, women and children. A few miles down the road they saw a group of Sikh horsemen riding out of tall grass along the road attacking another group of migrants with swords. He ordered his men to open fire, they fled back into the tall grass. Not wanting to leave these families, he started unloading the books and filling the trucks with people. At the end of their 31-mile journey, there was just one truck of books and nearly a thousand men, women and children.

In serious trouble with his superiors, he told them he would do it again if he had to and it was up to them to decide if the books were more important than the lives he saved. The decision in his favour, they handed him the R.P.A.F. Provost Unit on Ingle Road in Karachi to start the new Air Force Police Training School.

Several years later in 1978, Dad had retired from the Air Force and was now the Personnel Manager for National Motors, when one of the workers brought a grievance case against the company. Karachi at the time was under Martial Law, and when they were in court, the young Army Judge kept staring at Dad while the other cases were being presented. When their case finally came up, the judge got up from behind the bench, walked up to Dad and shook his hand, "You sir would be Uncle Harry. You won't recognise me, but I never forgot your face. I was one of those little boys you picked up and put into the back of a truck that fateful day in 1947. You saved my mother and grandparents and hundreds of others." He then proceeded to tell everyone in the courtroom the story of that horrific day and how Dad had rescued them. There were tears in his eyes when he was done. After listening in silence, the room burst into cheers. The judge threw Dad's case out, saying he was done for the day.

Mom and Dad married in 1954, had three kids, my sister Linda in 1955, brother Vivian in 1956 and me in 1963. Linda passed away at just 17 in 1973 from a massive heart attack. Dad retired from the Air Force after that, and we moved to the city.

Living on air bases across Pakistan, my parents had educated the children of all the staff working at our homes. Us kids were raised to look out for those less fortunate than us. It is my parents' influence that spurs me to do the same for my own staff, by fighting to have their kids educated in the private school where I taught, sitting alongside children of ministers and diplomats. I won my battle on their behalf. My brother and I continue to live our lives influenced by the example they set us.

In 2006, Dad was diagnosed with pulmonary fibrosis and given three months to live. He told the doctor "Doc you're talking bullshit, I'll live three years." He lived three-and-a-half more years, passing away on Linda's death anniversary in 2010. He was given a Police Honour Guard funeral by the Toronto Police.

A fighter throughout his life, he did things his way, and I can only dream of being a fraction of the man he was.

Michael's parents in 1954 a few months before their wedding

Lindsay W. Albert

Lindsay W. Albert was born to a bereaved Dad and Mum, less than a year after the sudden traumatic death of her infant sister. Lindsay began life having an intimate relationship with death despite her parents' efforts to shield her from dying and death. Not surprisingly, Lindsay's life journey has centred around helping and comforting others; this she does in many ways including through her writing and her career in palliative end of life care. Since 2013, Lindsay has published poems, prose and photography in numerous anthologies and in The Artis literary magazine.

Born to Rescue

A daughter was born
to parents elated
Three months of joy
then tragedy struck
leaving their hearts
unimaginably torn

Inconsolable was their grief
trauma shattered their world
"Have another baby" they're told
to distract from the pain
Soon another daughter was born
to bring relief and hope

Innately knowing her role
as defined in Mother's womb
via echoes of her parents' grief
sensing their broken hearts
She came to rescue her parents
from the grip of grief and trauma
She knew her life's mission
was to love and to console

Norma Nicholson

Norma Nicholson is a retired nurse with a BA in Sociology and Psychology and an MA in Adult Education. She recently completed four years as a highly engaged member of the Region of Peel Police Services Board. Norma is a three-time published author, who uses tools from her books to mentor and educate the vulnerable in communities through advocacy, motivational, public and keynote speaking. She was listed among the 100 Accomplished Black Canadian Women (100ABC Women) in 2018. Her website is normanicholson.ca

My Mother, My Father = Myself

Not really! My life took a different path, and so the title of my story should be:
My Grandmother = Myself

C.S Lewis says *"Hardships often prepare ordinary people for extraordinary destiny."*

At the age of two, I began to ask my grandma, Nana Francis about my mom and dad. She told me that I belonged to her; she was my mom and dad together. I truly did not understand what that meant. I lived with my 80-year grandmother on her farm where there were no children or any other household member. Living by herself in a remote village, she did everything to manage her household such as farming, shopping at the market, tending the animals and chopping wood for the wood-burning stove.

She built me wooden toy trucks and dolls which I loved to play with. I was also allowed to play in the gardens on the farmland and go with her to tend the animals. I enjoyed fresh fruits, vegetables, meat and milk from the farm. Adults from the surrounding villages came to visit my grandma on Saturdays to purchase some of these items. She then had money to purchase things such as clothes and shoes.

My grandmother could not read but she had a very large Bible on her bedside table. She would often open it and touched different pages while saying "God loves both of us." I silently wished I could read but had no one to teach me. Some children are fortunate to attend kindergarten and then advance to other grades as they got older. There was no school within ten miles of where we lived.

As I got older, I really wanted to find out about my parents and any other family member that I may have. When I was six-years-old, my grandmother revealed an amazing story of how I came to live with her. And she suggested what my life's potential would be. My precious gift of life was:

I was born to a teen mother who lived in abject poverty, she was unable to care for me after the age of six months. She had been dating my father who was twice her age and a married man. She found his home address and took me there and left me on the sidewalk. A police officer on duty walked by and saw this infant who was about to crawl into the street. He picked me up and noticed there was a note taped to my diaper which stated, "take your baby, I can no longer look after her."

The officer went to the address and rang the doorbell. Out came my stepmother who wanted to know why he was standing there with an infant. The officer explained that he had found me in the street at her address and then read the note to her. She was taken aback that her husband fathered a child outside of their marriage.

There was no Children's Aid Society or Social Worker they could call to come and take this infant. The officer suggested that he would work with his Police Division to find my mother and that my father's wife should try to take care of the infant until her husband arrived home from work. They both hoped that he would be able to provide added information and a contact for the child's mother.

Amazingly when my father arrived home, after a much-heated discussion with his wife, he confessed that he was the father of the infant and did not know where her mother lived. A plot was developed that no one should know what happened and the infant could be taken to the remote village where his mother (my grandmother) lived. This would ensure that she was living with someone who would love her and take good care of her and no one would know that he had an extramarital affair with a young girl.

Though my grandmother had done everything for me in love, I felt very sad that I was unwanted. I cried a lot, refused to eat and had a great desire to find my parents. My nana was so loving, she held me close to her body and hugged me for hours as she poured out much love and care to help me heal. Since I could not contact my parents, even at a young age, my desire was to learn how to read so that I could read the stories in my nana's Bible.

My dream to learn to read was realized soon after I was told why I lived with my grandmother. A lady, Ms. Livingston came from the 'big city' to teach at the local school due to a shortage of teachers in that area. Not only did she rent a room from my grandmother, she owned a car! I felt so blessed as she encouraged my nana to send me to school with her each day. There was no school library, but the teachers brought many old books for children to read. As I learned to read, I became more interested in learning and would pick up old magazines and newspapers around the school, take them home to read. I read even at night using a candle or by the light from a kerosene lantern.

My grandmother was so proud of me, she would listen when I read and when I found words that were difficult to read,

My dream was to learn to read ~ Norma

she would encourage me to spell out the words and try to pronounce them. She would tell me every morning that I was born for a purpose and I should learn as much as possible and be kind to everyone. She realized that at times I would become quite sad along with being very angry. Only someone who has experienced such life situations would understand how these two emotions would at times overtake me.

Sadly, my grandmother died when I was only eight years old. I slept beside her in a large oak bed and she would often awaken me if she needed to have a candle lit so she could go to the bathroom. On the night she died, she did not get up to go to the bathroom and when I touched her, she was very cold. I ran to awaken Ms. Livingston to ask her to come over to see my Nana. She confirmed that she had stopped breathing. She then drove into the small town where she informed folks of my Nana's death and she sent telegrams to those who lived in the 'big city.'

I wanted to die and go to heaven with my grandmother. I could not imagine how I could ever live without her. I met my father for the first time when he and other family members came to my grandmother's funeral. He and his wife had hidden me away for so many years, did not visit or even ask about me, yet I was happy to know that I had a father who was alive. I had heard my grandmother say that whenever I meet my father, I would find a piece of myself. My dad is a complete mystery. The only concern he had was where would I go to live now that his mom had died. I don't know how the arrangements were made but I found out that I would be moving to his older sister's home much further into the countryside.

A new life began in another family member's home. I am so thankful that I continued to learn and attend school. I underwent horrific abuses for the next five years. My aunt detested me and wished that I would die, therefore ensured access to only a few meals, little clothing or caring. I was a trooper as I continued to remember the love and mentorship I received from my grandmother. Ms. Livingston was no longer involved in my life, but I remembered the great stories she shared about obstacles which are opportunities to learn and become better.

As a teenager, I began to question my existence and decided to run away to find my father. Ms. Livingston shared his address and I walked for over three days to find him. I slept in the bushes, drank water from the streams and ate fruits along the paths. When I arrived at his home, his wife allowed me to stay. I was encouraged as I was able to attend school again and actively participate in life's adventures. My dad was now older and did not seem to care if I lived at this home as long as I kept out of his way.

My zest for life continues. My story has taught me to appreciate life as it were a gift you never want to give up. My philosophy to this day is change the way you do things and life will change for the better. I keep looking and moving forward and I deliver my best self each and every day.

I keep looking and moving forward and I deliver my best self each and every day.~ Norma Nicholson

Bev Bachmann

Bev Bachmann taught high school English in the Toronto/Peel areas until she retired and began a career in writing. Her first novel *Christmas Touches* is available on Amazon in print and e-book format. Her second novel *Student Body,* a murder mystery set in a Toronto high school, is available at the Friesen Press Bookstore.

Bev Bachmann

My Mother, My Father, My Step-Father = myself

Are we like our parents, or simply influenced by them? And does it matter if we are their natural offspring or rather the result of marital realities? Is the answer simply an offshoot of the nature versus nurture debate, or is it something else entirely???

My Mother...

I'll start by saying that my dearest hope is to be nothing like this woman who, in her 90's, is still a child. However, now that I'm in my sunset years, I sometimes wonder.

But to begin at the beginning—my mother was a pretty 18-year-old when she delivered me in St. Joseph's Hospital in Toronto, Ontario. We were strangers at the moment of my birth and were to remain so throughout my lifetime.

My Father...

I did have a physical father who was briefly married to my mother whom he met at a munitions factory during the War. Having accomplished his part in impregnating her, his eye was caught by another young girl, and he promptly moved on. That's really all I know about him, except for the one photo I have of him which reveals a certain cockiness that, for some unknown reason, makes me smile. I certainly never blamed him for leaving my mother for the woman whose name appears on their divorce papers. In my opinion, it was the smartest thing he ever did.

After the marriage break-up, the question came up of what to do about the baby? The answer was simple. Hand her over to the most convenient woman around—my mother's mother. And that is how I ended up in the home and the heart of a woman I truly did love. My Grandmother.

And all went well until fate brought on the scene an American G.I. who was touring Toronto on furlough in order to take in the CNE. During his stay, he happened to meet a petite, rather striking-looking young woman, and soon discovered that she had the quality he wanted most in a mate—malleability. And, as for her, she immediately recognized that here was her ticket out—out of Canada and into the Promised Land, where her American saviour would take care of her for the rest of her life. They were married within a week.

One night in April, four weeks before my sixth birthday, I am warm and safe under the covers in a bed I shared with my Grandmother. The next night I am sleeping on a Murphy bed in a ghetto in Detroit. I had no foreknowledge of the cataclysmic event that had just occurred. All I knew was that overnight I lost everything that mattered to me. *How did it happen?*

The woman who was my natural mother, but knew nothing about me except my name, had decided to yank me out of my real home and take me across the border to Michigan where she would wait for her new American husband to join her. Why did she do it? My guess was to keep her from being lonely in a new

Bev with her Grandmother

country where she knew no one else. It's just a guess, of course, but probably as good a guess as any.

Suddenly I understood the despair of a caged animal. But what could I do about it? The law was on her side. As my biological mother, she had the power of possession. She owned my body. But not my mind. My sole focus became one of survival. I began to map out strategies for staying alive until I could reach the legal age of 18. Nothing else mattered.

As a six-year-old, I had seen that it was possible to lose the only person you love. I had to find a way to keep that from happening again. The only solution I came up with in my child's mind was to never love again. It was the only way I could think of to keep from dying.

In the twelve years that I lived with my mother and her husband, I never cried. Tears were useless. Feelings were useless. I had to become invisible. It was my main strategy for survival.

One day I was in a clothing store and absentmindedly staring at a rack of sweaters when a bright young salesclerk breezed by and suddenly stopped in her tracks. She turned to me and said, "I thought you were a mannequin." I smiled at her and let her show me stuff I didn't really need. She was sweet and funny and endearing. I remember thinking to myself, 'if only she knew how right she was.'

So, the question remains: did I turn out to be like my mother? A woman whose selfishness was matched only by her shallowness? I can't say for sure. There have been moments throughout my life when I was insensitive, like the time I tried to secretly win over my girlfriend's sweetheart and never told her about it. Fortunately, I was unsuccessful in the attempt, but was that any different from my mother stealing me away from the person I loved? Only by degrees.

Maybe my mother was right when she used to repeatedly call me "good for nothing." When I thought about it rationally, her pronouncements didn't make sense. I was the one who took care of the dinner, the laundry, the ironing, the vacuuming, and the babysitting of her other kid, my little half-sister.

"Good for nothing?" Really?

So, was I like her? I admit to being more than a little judgmental, but I never said anything remotely like that to any of my high school students, whatever their intellectual abilities. They were people. Just like me.

As for my mother, I can't help but wonder what kind of woman would tear a child away from the only home she had ever known and imprison her with strangers of questionable sanity? I honestly don't know. What I do know is no power on earth would make me do something like that.

My step-father

My step-father, in the beginning, did try to act like a real father. We were introduced when I was six, and it seemed to me, he actually liked me. He often took me to the air base where he worked so he could show me off to his colleagues. He entertained me by showing me how the 'ancient' teletype machine worked and introduced me to the other GIs who seemed to find me charming.

We had fun together, and I think the memory of those early days stayed with us as the years went on as the atmosphere in the home became increasingly toxic.

So, was I like him? He was tough and his rages could be terrifying. I saw him scare people who, more often than not, gave him a wide berth. I did too, although he didn't scare me. For all of my high school years, I stayed sequestered in my room where I was deeply engrossed in homework.

The one thing I could count on with my step-father was his high regard for education. If I was doing homework, then, not only would he leave me alone, he actually encouraged the long hours I would spend in my room studying my heart out. He himself had only a high school education, and he had seen how it had limited his adult life. So, I understood how much he valued education. In his way, he respected me. But that didn't stop his constant criticism or episodes of manic behaviour or even of standing in the doorway of my bedroom in the middle of the night with a menacing look on his face.

It was all a game. He wanted to break me. It didn't happen. I think he was obsessed with getting my respect because he knew he didn't have it. And it drove him crazy. Literally. He didn't seem to want my mother's respect. He saw her for what she was.

I know he thought when he and I first met that my mother and I had had a "normal mother-daughter" relationship. He didn't know that, from the time I was born, I had seen her on only three occasions and each time for a matter of minutes. He didn't know that she and I had never bonded. He actually believed that I thought of her as my mother. Why should he think any differently?

Over and over, he kept trying to impress upon me that we were 'a family.' When I was about eight, my mother told me that my step-father was really my biological father. I found this totally confusing. So, where was he the first six years of my life, I asked her. "Overseas," she said. The American government didn't allow wives to accompany their husbands overseas, she lied. I believed her. I was eight.

Then one day when I was 17, my step-father told me the truth. He did it to get back at his wife during one of their epic fights. I believe he was tired of the deception and I suspect that somewhere deep in his psyche there was an honourable person.

Today he is buried somewhere in Sacramento, California, and it's too late for me to tell him anything. We were never a family. My mother lied to him just as she had lied to me. And, the fact of the matter is she hurt him. Hurt him deeply. Like me, my step-father valued the truth, and for that reason alone, I do, indeed, respect him.

And as for my mother—do I respect her? The woman used me as a domestic servant, filled my head with despicable lies, and destroyed my desire—but not my ability—to love.

In short, she blighted my life until the day I took back control by going to university, getting a teaching degree, and re-uniting with my beloved Grandmother. So, do I forgive her? Well, I'll leave the final word to the ghost of Hamlet's father:

"Leave her to heaven."

Harvinder Kaur Dhillon

Harvinder Kaur Dhillon is of South Asian origin, born and raised in Nairobi, Kenya, and holds Canadian and British citizenship. She is currently retired in Kasauli, Himachal Pradesh, India. In collaboration with her daughter, Jasteena Dhillon, she is working on her family history due to be published in 2020 through Diamond Legacies/IOWI. An excerpt from the manuscript is submitted here.

Harvinder Kaur Dhillon

He did what a father had to do

My father was born in the village of Sohian in Ludhiana, British India. He was one of three siblings and the most ambitious of them. He was very clever and a bit of a non-conformist. He studied in Ludhiana, Punjab, India. He died when I was very young, but I was regaled with stories of his strength and courage.

Since his father and grandfather did not have much land, my father (Bhauji) was told that as his family had spent money on his studies, he would not be given any land. All the property would go to his older brother. My father was enraged by this decision and left home. He ended up in Bombay and boarded the first outgoing ship that happened to be going to Mombasa in East Africa. How he survived the journey I don't know, but he landed in Mombasa alone and penniless. He was 24-years-old at the time.

From Mombasa he ended up going to Nairobi, which is the capital of Kenya. Since he was educated and spoke English (which was rare at the time), he managed to get a job as a teacher in a government school. He was also a translator for Indian troops under the British army and posthumously received an award from the Queen for his commitment to the war effort. I am so proud of him.

Bhauji was a strict teacher but took personal interest in the education of his students. He was well-regarded by that entire generation that he taught, and for many years after, his reputation as an excellent teacher held among his students wherever they went. I continue to meet his students till today and they still speak highly of him. They say that they are doctors and lawyers and engineers because of my dad's interest in them.

Being ambitious, Bhauji saved money and bought a house in Nairobi. Later I was told that he was well-known for having people stay with him rent-free, till they could afford to pay. Word got around in Ludhiana that my father would accommodate newcomers free of charge in Nairobi till they got a job. He earned a very good reputation and was well-loved and respected in the community.

Then at the age of 29, he decided to get married. He wrote a letter to his friend in India, asking him to find him a suitable match as he would be travelling to India soon. When he got to India, his friend suggested his own sister who like my father was also educated. Though she was barely 15 years old at the time, my father married Biji.

My mother, Biji, travelled to Kenya with my father, Bhauji, leaving her family behind. A year into their marriage, they had a baby girl who was like a porcelain doll with delicate, fine features. She was the apple of my father's eye. My parents, Biji and Bhauji, had nine more children after that.

Bhauji was aware of his eldest daughter's beauty and decided it would be best to get her married soon after puberty and started looking for a match as soon as she was 15 years old. Lots of suitors came forward. A prominent family was chosen. The family consisted of three brothers and two sisters, the intended groom being the middle brother. He was a strapping young lad

Harvinder's parents: Bauji and Biji

with a powerful voice and personality.

Bhauji gave a big dowry to his lovely daughter. A cash settlement was also put in a joint account with himself. The wedding was the talk of the town.

Biji was distraught because her precious daughter was going to Kijavi, a village far away where the family lived. They were a family of hunters and made their living by selling tusks and animal skins. They were quite well off. The father was semi-retired and the three boys took over the hunting and were away in the jungle for weeks at a time and the women in the household (mother, two daughters and daughters-in-law) were left to fend for themselves.

My sister adjusted well in the family. Her mother-in-law was very fond of her and taught her all the fineries of life: cooking, sewing and knitting. My sister used to visit Nairobi quite infrequently to be with us, her siblings. Once in a while when her husband, my brother-in-law, was home, they would both come and stay in Nairobi for days.

They were a very happy couple and very much in love. The only drawback was that after a year of marriage, my sister had not conceived and she was distraught about it. It was a great worry to her and she became quite obsessed with having a baby.

Whenever she came to Nairobi, she would complain to Biji that she did not like her father in-law's behaviour towards her, as he would taunt her that she was barren. Biji did not want Bhauji to know this because she knew he would be infuriated. So, she went with my sister and confronted the father-in-law. This did not work—in fact, things became worse. He became more blatant in his taunts and whenever they were in contact, he would ask her to let him have his way with her. My sister was very scared of the dirty old man and would avoid him at all cost. Her mother-in-law knew all about it but turned a blind eye towards it.

In desperation, my sister told her husband what was going on and he became very angry and confronted the old man, at which the predator became bolder. While the sons had gone hunting, he tried to knock down my sister's bedroom door but was unsuccessful. This really scared her, so when the boy came home, she told him what had happened. In a fit of anger, the boy gave my sister a gun and told her if he tried to do that again, to "**shoot the bastard**." The gun was kept in a bedside locker.

Sure enough, when the sons had gone hunting, the father-in-law knocked down the door of my sister's bedroom and entered. My sister took out the gun and shot him once. He started towards her saying "what have you done." She was so scared that she shot two more bullets into his body and he fell down. Petrified at seeing him lying on the floor in a pool of blood, she started screaming and ran out of the room.

Meanwhile, the household woke. My sister threw the gun into a pit and told them that an intruder had broken the door open and had shot the father.

The police were summoned. My sister was arrested for premeditated murder. When news got to Bhauji, he, Bibi and others immediately set off for the police station. When they saw their frightened daughter, she was so distraught that she fainted in my mother's arms.

After regaining consciousness, she narrated the whole tale to her parents in the presence of the police. Bhauji's response was that he would have done the same and he hugged his daughter.

Since the conversation was in Punjabi, the African policemen did not comprehend what was being said.

Meanwhile my brothers were busy procuring a lawyer and brought him to the police station. Though the lawyer told them to concoct a story, Bhauji refused. He wanted the truth to be known.

My brother-in-law was also there to support his wife, but Bhauji asked him to leave and blamed him for not protecting his daughter from the monster. Till his dying day, he did not talk to his son-in-law.

Bhauji left no stone unturned to get the best counsel for his daughter. All of Nairobi's prominent citizens rallied around the family and my sister. Yet, there were those who also belittled my sister and smeared her character as well. Especially the boy's family who accused her of having affairs (in a jungle, imagine!). The trial date was set.

Bhauji was in Court every day and was very distraught seeing his fragile daughter in the dock. She was very weak and was losing a lot of weight and also fainted in the dock a few times during the trial. The boy's family used a lot of false evidence against my sister. The judge patiently listened to all the evidence. After the trial, the judgment was very prompt. She was declared guilty and the punishment was death by hanging.

Bhauji appealed the sentence. He sought out a prominent lawyer in the United Kingdom. To pay for all the trial expenses, Bhauji had to sell one of his properties.

The Scottish lawyer was very competent and did his best. He wanted to appeal to the King for a pardon. The whole of Nairobi rallied around the family going door to door to collect signatures of citizens to gain a pardon for my sister. There was an overwhelming response and thousands of signatures were collected and sent to London to the King of England.

The King reduced the sentence to life imprisonment—which was a bit of relief to our family.

The prison was far away from Sikh colony, so our family tried to visit my sister if not every day then every other day. Bhauji used to have talks with my sister and always asked the same thing as to why she did not confide in him because he would have sorted out the situation.

My sister was treated like a special prisoner. She was given quarters next to the warden. She was not in the general prison but had her own bedroom, living room, bathroom and garden.

The warden, Mr Smith and his wife had two teenaged daughters. Mrs Smith and her daughters were very fond of my sister and came and sat with her often. She could wear her own clothes and not the prisoners' garb. My sister used to teach the warden's girls to sew, knit and embroider.

I remember going to visit her with Biji. It was a long, long walk and Biji would go loaded with goodies for my sister and Mrs Smith would treat us to tea.

My sister was very fond of me. I was six years old at the time and one day she begged Bhauji to let me stay with her. Unbeknownst to the authorities, I was asked to hide under the bed when the guard came in the evening. It was an adventure for me. The next day my brother came and took me home.

My sister adjusted well in the prison, but grew frailer and frailer. She was just skin and bones and developed some health issues. She was hospitalized a few times.

Life in our household began to return to as normal as possible under the circumstances. The siblings who were in school were taunted all the time and they were reluctant to go to school. Bhauji also withdrew from society and kept to himself.

My sister developed a chronic problem and was hospitalized for a long period of time. She had only spent six months in jail by that time. Then one day, a police jeep arrived at the family residence. In the jeep were two policemen and between them was a frail-looking girl. My sister had been released. Joy radiated through the household and neighbourhood. *Methai* [ed. *sweets*] was distributed in the neighbourhood. My sister WAS FREE!

After about a month in our family home, my sister decided to reunite with her husband, who had stood by her, to start their own life together. By this time the boy had spilt from his family as a way to demonstrate his love for my sister. He was working and had a flat of his own. Reluctantly, Bhauji let my sister go with him, vowing never to see them again. My sister still used to come and visit her family unbeknownst to Bhauji.

Bhauji took early retirement from teaching and was quite happy being at home. He focused on his real estate business and began making frequent trips to India as well to buy property there. Biji, my mother, was content to be at home looking after the family as well as the properties, collecting rent.

I was twelve-years-old when suddenly Bhauji suffered a massive brain haemorrhage. Doctors were summoned but could not save him. He died without reconciling with his daughter. But his sense of family and 'doing what you had to do' is something that is ingrained in the minds of each member of his large family.

Kildeer chicks
Photo credit: Merridy Cox

Sharon Berg

Sharon Berg writes poetry, story, book reviews, and nonfiction that focuses on First Nations history and education. She was very active in the literary community. She has a B.A in Native Studies, a B.Ed., an M.Ed. and a D.Ed. She worked as an elementary school teacher and retired in 2016. Sharon founded Big Pond Rumours International Literary Zine in 2006 which ran till 2019. Big Pond press continues and publishes chapbooks by Canadian authors. She lives in Sarnia, Ontario.

A Mother's Patience

I knew that a proper mother would not say certain things. Proper being the term for acquiescence, for accepting blame, for all things being the fault of the wilful girl who broke society's rules and defied her parents. Except that wasn't really my story.

"When I finally met her, she was a different sort of fruit than I expected. That's for sure. There's this old saying: A melon forced off its vine is not as sweet. Maybe that applies to a child who is forced to grow up without her mother. To grow up without connection to her birth mother, I mean. She was fully formed as a human being by the time I met her at age thirty-nine. We aren't talking about a child."

I was referring to my adopted daughter. Or rather, the child I'd given up for adoption when I was a teenager. I was referring to that old pain, the one that scarred so deeply it never left me. Cynthia had been my friend for at least two decades. She was my confidante, though we didn't always agree.

"You're being cruel now, aren't you, Elke?" she said now. "You're talking about your own flesh and blood, after all."

Cynthia's shockingly clear blue eyes registered disapproval. She had no ideal what it felt like to give up a child as I had.

"Sure, I am. Clearly you're disregarding the studies into the effect of nature versus nurture. I don't apologize for holding to my own opinion. Neither one of us would fudge the truth."

"I just don't know how you can speak like that about someone you birthed."

I hadn't seen Cynthia in days. She was becoming exasperated by me, or by my part in this conversation, I should say.

My friend was a naturally kind-hearted person, someone who never spoke ill of anyone else, who was always clear-sighted. Her negative opinions were simply not expressed. This was not true of me any longer. I understood her position. It was the same one I'd held until my suspicions about Jemma began to grow. My thoughts had definitely changed after Jemma revealed her true self. I'd met her about ten years earlier. She'd introduced herself through email as the person I'd given-up for adoption.

Part of this was my own fault, admittedly. That introduction by email had flagged down a woman who'd simply pined for her child since they were released through adoption. I fell for her line right away. Wanting to meet my long-lost child with all of my being, I let my guard down. I invited her into my life immediately. It was only as time passed that I realized several things about her just didn't add up. I had questions that I could find no answer for.

"I never thought I would say this about anyone, Cynthia, but Jemma has proven herself to be incredibly manipulative and spiteful. All of that was not apparent on our first meeting, of course. She fooled me then. I see it in the way that things have developed over time."

"Think about your own actions, though. You welcomed her with open arms when you first met. You invited her to be a part of your family. Then, just three weeks later, you pulled the rug out from under her by saying you didn't want further contact. All of that is further complicated by the fact that she still has contact with your other children."

Cynthia didn't know all of the ins and outs of this situation. She didn't understand why I rejected her approach to the person who claimed she was my child. The idea that you should hold your tongue if you have ill thoughts about someone went with the old me, the person I was before I met Jemma. I was learning over time; learning hard.

"Am I, really as bad as she is?" I asked. "I think that—assuming she's my child—she wanted retribution and she took it, without giving me a chance to explain why I gave her up for adoption. I have paid full price now, in my sixties, for a decision I made at the age of seventeen... on her behalf. Fifty years ago, it wasn't only single parents who suffered socially but their children. In my mind, the best thing, the most loving thing I could do for my child was to arrange that she received two parents. If I couldn't give that to her on my own—and I couldn't—I did the next best thing, giving her up for adoption at birth. In my understanding, those were the children who had the best chance of growing up fully loved and adored."

"I understand that. I agree with you, Elke. In fact, I think you chose a really difficult path in giving her up like that. I know things were really different back then. I just don't think you should speak this way about her now. Words have power. You're imprinting this negative impression of her on your own mind, and it may not be true."

"There are things you don't realize, Cynthia. Things that slipped past me at our first meeting. When Nia had trouble with her hips with Legg-Calve-Perthes disease, around the age of four, and she had twisted bones in her legs, I wrote to the Children's Aid. I wanted to find out how Jemma had managed, if she'd developed any significant childhood diseases. The information I received came in a letter. I still have it. It told me non-identifying things such as she was healthy, had no significant childhood illnesses outside of the ordinary, and she was blonde with brown eyes. You've seen Jemma. That doesn't describe her.

"No, she has dark brown hair," Cynthia agreed, "but hair colour can change over time. It happened with my older brother. He was blond as a baby and developed dark hair later."

"Fine," I said, nodding. "I know that can happen. But the colour of people's eyes doesn't change like that. Jemma has blue eyes. I don't think she is my child. And the birth date is wrong."

"What?" Her face registered shock. "So you have two reasons for doubting she is your child?"

"Yeah, at least two. For me, there's a third reason as well."

"Okay." Cynthia was clearly beginning to shift away from not speaking about my negative thoughts. "Explain it."

"First, her birth date is wrong. She insists her birthday is May 26th. I gave birth to my baby on May 5th. You know that date was seared into my memory. I don't think there is a mother on the planet who would forget the day her first child is born."

Cynthia sat quietly for a moment. "There must be some explanation."

"Suggest one to me. How does one get the birth date wrong? You know what she said to me? 'You just got confused.' Really? I pined for my child. I have never forgotten the day she was born, or the details of her birth. I don't think that Jemma is my child, Cynthia."

"Don't say that," she whispered, shaking her head.

"Why not? Because it upsets the apple cart? Because it interferes with the pretty portrait we have of the Children's Aid and happy-ever-after family reunions?"

"It's just…" she left the end of that sentence unspoken.

"I wrote to the Children's Aid, you know. I told them about my reservations and gave them Jemma's name, which is not the name I gave to my child."

"Her parents likely changed her name. And maybe they decided to celebrate the day that they received her as her birthday."

"Sure, I considered all of that. But I wrote to the Children's Aid. Do you know what their response was?"

Cynthia simply shook her head.

"They told me that I'd gotten myself confused about which day I gave birth to my child. Their response was so patronizing I still shake with anger over it. It was absolutely infuriating. I think it is far more likely that they have mistakes in their paperwork. We all know babies are sometimes switched at birth in hospitals. Why can that not happen in the case of a baby's paperwork at Children's Aid? I know, with utter certainty, that I gave birth on May 5th. Earlier information from CAS told me she had brown eyes."

"So who are you angry with? Jemma or the Children's Aid?"

"Do I have to choose? I'm looking at her current actions, her current influence on my other daughters. She's chosen to play a part in separating my other children, her sisters, from me as their mother. How does that serve their best interests? Neither one of them will talk to me now. I can only think it all comes back to Jemma."

Cynthia was still shaking her head, "You can't say that. You can't mean that. You raised two beautiful and intelligent girls. They'd never be fooled by someone as manipulative as you're suggesting Jemma is."

"Right. And all daughters love their mothers, and all mothers love their daughters, come kingdom high! Nothing shall ever cleave them apart."

Cynthia sat back with an expression of distaste for the place our conversation had come to. She threw her hands in the air in a gesture to demonstrate that she gave up.

"But it comes back to that whole question of nature or nurture, doesn't it?" I continued. "I mean, how much of each—inherited traits or experience—makes the person who they are? What is it about experiences that tend to mould a series of behaviours, more than the inherited genetics?"

"Elke, you're talking about your own child! Do you actually believe in the depth of your heart that she isn't yours?"

"Yes." I paused to give emphasis to my point. "I believe that's a distinct possibility. I had a child and I gave her up for adoption. CAS didn't live up to any of their promises to me. I was told she'd go to a dentist with a stay-at-home wife who was a painter, a watercolourist. But Jemma went to a factory worker whose wife was a grocery cashier.

"We know CAS have done some horrible things, not properly tracking what happened with children they put into the care of people who turned out to be abusers or pedophiles. I have to say I pined for my girl every day after her birth. I worried about her, wondering what her life was like, wondering if she'd even survived at times."

"What do you mean, 'if she had even survived'? You thought she might not?"

"I'm not being melodramatic. Truly. I knew there was a greater chance that she was fine, that she had prospered. That's the whole reason I'd given her up, to give her a better chance of doing well in life. My own prospects were pretty terrible at that point. My parents wanted to send me away to have the baby, but I'd heard horror stories about babies born in homes for unwed mothers being sold on the black market. Plus, as we know, all sorts of kids—from good families or struggling ones—lose their way and get into drugs or alcohol. There were reports that surfaced about adoptive families that were clearly failures. I just didn't know. I had no way to check what had happened to her."

"Ah, I understand."

"That whole thing about childhood trauma and PTSD, though... The point I'm trying to make is, a child can suffer PTSD just as easily as an adult, maybe more easily. You know there are studies that prove—over the past twenty years or so—that childhood trauma actually affects the development of a child's brain."

"I know, I was reading something about that. So you're thinking that a child in foster care, or an adopted child, goes through trauma, correct?"

"Not quite as directly as that. Not all foster care situations are terrible, but some of them definitely are. And yes, an adopted child could have a terrible experience. On my first meeting with her, Jemma told me she loved her adoptive father. She said no one could have had a better dad. But her mother and grandmother were a different story. She said they used to beat her with wooden spoons or a belt. I know what that's like. She grew up hating her adoptive mother and grandmother. What I don't get is how she could have made her mind up about me, dismissing me and trashing me to my other children, in the two months we were still talking."

"Two months. That's it?"

"Pretty much. Three meetings over two months."

"What happened to change things at the point of two months?"

"That's when Nia told me some things Jemma had said to her, which made it pretty clear she wanted to severe my girls from me. The biggest thing was the way she started telling both Nia and Ava that she felt sorry for them, simply because they were raised by me."

"What?"

"Yeah, she thought that my raising them had put them through all kinds of needless trauma, that I had subjected them to things no child should live through."

"Really? How would she have known that? Where did she get this information?"

"Well, all I can tell you is she certainly didn't know me from the three short visits we had during those same two months. She always put on a smiling face when she was around me, but that is not what she presented to my other daughters. It made me regret ever giving her the contact information for my girls. I was too trusting."

"Have you told the girls what you suspect? That Jemma isn't their sister?"

"Yes, I listed my reasons why, as well. They took the same attitude you did at first, that I was being a terrible mother to suggest anyone could pretend to be another person, as Jemma has."

"So they don't believe you?"

"No, and now they have cut me out of their lives. I can't see my grandchildren or visit with them. They refuse to respond to email messages and they've blocked my phone number. They chose Jemma over their mother."

"I can't believe those girls would do such a thing. They've cut you right out of their lives? They're too sensible for that. Those girls loved you."

"They did. Now, apparently, they don't. I'm certain that is Jemma's influence."

"I'm so sorry, Elke. What do you plan to do?"

"What can I do? I can just continue to live my life, is all. Just carry on as before. There are years ahead of us and I have patience. Sooner or later, Jemma will grow dissatisfied with the situation. She'll begin to make mistakes, and my two brilliant girls will start to assemble them, piecing together the bigger story, just as I have."

"It is a mistake to try to step between a mother and her children," Cynthia commented. "You've said that before."

"Yes. And I was proven right. Its a good thing that I have patience. I would do anything for my kids, but I won't beg for their attention. I'll wait for them to see Jemma as I do. Maybe I shouldn't say this out loud, but if I keep writing and publishing, sooner or later my personal dream will be answered. I'll be contacted through my website by my long-lost daughter, the same way Jemma found me. But next time I'll keep my head when I'm contacted. I'll check her eye colour and her birth date before I accept her into my heart. Only after I am certain will I give out contact information for her sisters. A hard lesson has been learned."

"So you think you'll be contacted again?"

"Yes. It's one of the main reasons I've struggled to be an author people know.

I've always felt my child should be able to find me through my website."

Cynthia smiled, understanding.

Lina Alhabahbeh

Lina Alhabahbeh immigrated from Jordan to Canada in 2013. She holds a Bachelor's degree in Physical Education and was a PE teacher and coach in various sports for kids with and without disabilities. She currently works for the Peel District School Board. She has written and published literary pieces in Kuwait and Canada and has published a kids' book on Alzheimer's entitled *Sam and his Grandad*, IOWI, 2018.

Nostalgia

My dreams are heavy with longing
as harvest vineyards of grapes
olives and fragrant lemon trees
The sound of my mother's voice
carries through the window of the past
As does the bursts of laughter
from my dad, brothers and sisters
echo in the garden of my heart

Other memories
My grandmother's tales
My swing hanging from an almond tree
And how first love grew

And the promises of childhood…
of love, laughter
rise up nostalgically

Mom … dad
I am that spoiled child that you indulged
without conditions and without limits
You gave me wings to fly
held me when I faltered
You made me the girl
who is rattled by life
yet refuses to break.

I think about you all the time
How I need your advice
to carry me through the burdens in life
and soothe this longing
for those carefree days

Why didn't you warn me, show me
that life is not always easy, beautiful,
and free for the taking.

I. B. Iskov

I.B. (Bunny) Iskov is the Founder of The Ontario Poetry Society, theontariopoetrysociety.ca. Her poetry has been published in several literary journals and anthologies and she has won a few poetry contests. Most recently, Bunny had one of her poems published in *Tamaracks, Canadian Poetry for the 21ST Century*, Lummox Press. She is the 2009 recipient of the *R.A.V.E. Award* (Recognizing Arts Vaughan Excellence) and in 2017, she received the Absolutely Fabulous Woman Award for women over 40, for her contribution to the literary arts in the Golden Horseshoe.

Mother to Me

in memory of my mother Claire Hershberg

For decades
mother laboured
long and hard.
Delivered inseams and back seams,
stifled in sweltering sweatshops.

Her union never went on strike.

Mother lamented
she never owned a doll.

I was her doll,
her perfect goddess
even after braces,
three eye operations,
and breast surgery.

My mother to me
was like a block of wood,
sturdy and porous
while I was her conjured carving.

(*In A Wintered Nest*, Serengeti Press, 2013)

Ballet Lessons

Before I went to kindergarten
before I could roller skate
before I could read the time
before I could sing the alphabet
before I had anything else but baby teeth
I could dance ballet

Perfectly

I would raise my arms above my head in an arc
I would gracefully stand on my tiptoes
and pirouette
and pirouette
and pirouette
and pirouette
across Kildonan and Main
when the light was red
and my mother would scream my name
and run after me
and get hit by the car
and almost die.

(*Sapphire Seasons*, Aeolus House, 2010)

I.B. Iskov's parents: Claire & Jay C. Hershberg

Pressed for Space

"Ironing is a lost art"
some say in dry-clean tones.

I remember the simple life
when you could hang anything on the line,
let the summer wind
hug sheets and towels.

While mother scrubbed tired linoleum,
the radio played Patti Page.
Crinolines waltzed
at 33 and 45 revolutions per minute.

Wringing and wringing,
folding and folding
in permed bleached tight curls,
pedal pushers and bobby socks.

Cars stretched for miles
without a wrinkle.

Today, I iron shirts
to save money;
take the cordless phone off the hook,
hang sticky notes on my PC,
defrost chicken in the microwave.

Press my face
into your perma-press blue collar,
remember when life was simpler.

(*Sapphire Seasons*, Aeolus House, 2010)

Gurudas Gulwadi

Gurudas Gulwadi grew up at Kumta, a small coastal town in Karnataka State. He received a degree in Electrical Engineering from Pune University. He worked in India till retirement and then worked another ten years in the U.S. He now lives in Canada. He has a keen interest in writing and published a collection of poems and stories entitled *Musings on Life*, IOWI/DL, 2019.

My Father—Shripad

My father, Shripad, was born in the year 1900. But he was born ahead of his time. I realized that from my twenties onward, when I began to feel his influence in my life.

My father though intelligent did not get the proper grounding of formal education beyond primary school as there was no school near their home. He and his siblings were taught at home by his father—my grandfather, Manjunath. In later years, he would recall the corporal punishment he and his siblings often received from his father. He never resorted to this himself while raising his large family in trying times.

Manjunath had a keen interest in all things mechanical. He could open and repair wall clocks and timepieces. Watching him, Shripad got hooked on mechanical workings of things and soon he began helping his father. Father and son soon developed a skill set to make brass wheel cutting teeth in new material using a tool kit. They were soon able to repair a damaged wall clock by making new parts.

Once, Manjunath saw his British boss reading a book about homemade soap-making techniques. He borrowed the book for two or three weekends and copied the entire book on foolscap paper. Together with his two sons, Manjunath began making soap at home both for bodywash and for clothes. Once satisfied with the quality, he started selling the soaps to supplement the family's income.

My father learned how to cook from his mother Lalita and often helped her with the cooking whenever she was not well. And especially during the festivals where large quantities of special dishes and sweets had to be made. His mother was a great cook and this training was to stand him in good stead in later years when he started a restaurant.

Shripad's exposure to science and technology through his father, together with soap-making and doing odd mechanical jobs ensured a regular income for him. When he was twenty-four, his marriage was arranged to my mother, Shanti, who was only twelve at the time. Early marriage for girls was a norm in those days. So was joint-family system which provided financial stability.

With philosophical discourses taking place regularly at Shirali, its benevolent influence grew on Shripad. He also procured a new set of mechanical tools and honed his skills. He could easily make new components when required. He started repairing gadgets of the local people earning some extra money. When his eldest son started going to school, he crafted a cute school bag for his books using plywood and polishing it to a beautiful finish.

Manjunath breathed his last in 1938. I was born one year later, an eighth child. Shripad always believed that I was Manjunath, born again.

With his father's passing away, the pension stopped. The expenses did not. They were rising with the needs of a growing family. Shripad lacked any qualification, not even high school. He thought of going into business and decided on a restaurant. The restaurant "Sharada Bhuvan" began operations in the summer of 1940. Sharada was Shanti's name after marriage. Shripad lent a hand to the site workers and carpenters in many activities given his skill with tools.

My earliest memory of my father was at the age of five. I used to visit him in the evening around 5pm at the restaurant. He would be sitting with a few friends discussing the Second World War and India's freedom movement.

Gurudas' parents wedding--Shripad and Shanti
(his grandmother Lalita is seated extreme left)

At a friend's suggestion, Shripad began an apiary. Whenever the honeycombs brimmed with honey, he would borrow a gadget from his friend to extract the honey. Then, when the restaurant was not busy, I saw him working on a small machine for honey extraction. He fabricated the parts of the extractor painstakingly to create a machine that was much superior the one he used to borrow.

He loaded the four honeycombs heavy with honey into the housings of the stand in the machine and rotated the handle. Lo and behold, the honey started splashing out by centrifugal force along the inner walls of the machine. I stood proudly along with the children clapping at this amazing machine created by my father. When we reported this to our mother, she pointed out two other items he had 'invented' some years back both fabricated from brass sheet: one was a vegetable grater for carrot, beetroot, tomato, etc. The other piece was an exquisite oil dispenser. It looked like a magical Aladdin lamp!

By 1946, the restaurant business began to decline due to Shripad's blind trust in his cousin who was handling cash in his absence and two servants who were stealing grocery items like cooking oil.

I might have been seven or eight at the time, when one late afternoon I went to the restaurant. Shripad was sitting alone behind the cash drawer. He seemed relaxed as if in meditation. He gave me a hug and took me on his lap.

He smiled asking, "Whose father, am I?"

I answered, "You are my father."

Father: "You agree we are two separate beings?"

I: "Yes, I do."

Then he touched my shirt and said, "Whose shirt is this?"

I: "It is my shirt."

Father: "You agree, your shirt is different from you?"

I: "Yes, I do."

Next, he held my hand asking: "Whose hand is this?"

I: "It is my hand."

Father: "Gurudas, now let's see. You first agreed that you are different from me. Then you said your shirt and you are different. Isn't it?"

I: "Yes."

Father: "Similarly, you are different from your hand. You are not your hand nor are you your body. You may not understand it now. But remember it! One day you will."

These words stayed with me through the years. Much later when I was introduced to Vedantic concepts, I was struck by the fact that the Upanishadic core philosophy was what my father Shripad had referred to on that late afternoon in 1946.

My father had a great interest in reading newspapers to search for the latest news in science and technology. He would share what he thought was interesting and sometimes his comments would be futuristic. Once, maybe in 1948, he said, "A day will come when an appliance will be invented that will look like a dressing table with controls. By controlling the knobs, you will be able to talk and see a person in a distant place." His words indeed turned out to be prophetic. The video conference era began in the 1980s. FaceTime is commonplace now. Even today, I wonder how he thought of it, given the fact that regional language dailies in those days touched on science news in general, but hardly in depth.

My father was diagnosed with tuberculosis and passed away in April 1951. The restaurant went out of business by then and our family survived on remittances from the older sons who worked in big cities.

In retrospect, I think there were surely more Shripads born ahead of their time. They were not fortunate to have had the benefit of an education nor were they astute enough to understand the importance of overseeing in business. A brilliant mind full of promise just withered away. He was just fifty years old when he passed away.

God, I thank you for giving me Shripad!

My Mother–Shanti

My mother Sharada (née Shanti) was born in 1912 at Shirali, married my father in 1924 and lived twenty-four years longer than my father. She held all fifteen of her grandchildren in her lifetime. My mother knew great deprivation in her life. Her father, Atmaram, worked in a judicial office, and died very young leaving behind a wife and four children. Shanti, the eldest, was just eight at that time. She studied up to 4th grade as was usual at the time.

Being a bride, even before her teens, she was well taken care of by her in-laws, Manjunath and Lalita. These were the happiest days of my mother's life. Shripad was earning some money doing different odd jobs with his skill sets. As did my father, my mother too was influenced by the philosophical talks at home around the teachings of Swami Vivekananda and Vidyaranya. We, their children, were exposed to these learnings in our growing years.

Sharada's days of poverty began again with the declining fortune of the restaurant 'Sharada Bhuvan' and Shripad's illness. The family livelihood depended on money orders from my eldest brother who left for Bombay in 1947. After Shripad's demise in 1951, she started rolling out papads [ed. *papadums*] for the families in the neighbourhood to supplement income. She tried retrieving money from those who had taken meals at our restaurant on credit, but she could not retrieve a single paisa!

Sharada would often despair at our father's failure to provide for the future provision of his growing family. "What is the use of all those skills if children can't be fed," she would say, wringing her hands. She held the fort for eight long years from 1951 to 1959. Things were easier for her when her children grew up, began working and sending money home.

Gurudas' grandmother Sharada Shanti

Peter Reid

Peter Reid is married and lives with his wife on a small lake in West Quebec. Trained as an accountant, he realized, eventually, that he was an entrepreneur dressed in accountant's clothes. Until 2019, he allocated his time to mentoring entrepreneurs, gardening and raising goats and chickens, and helping poor communities around the world achieve their God-given potential. A lifelong avid fisherman, Peter published a memoir entitled *Diamonds on the Water—Waters I have fished, Lessons I have learned*, Diamond Legacies/IOWI, 2019. Peter says: "Each person has a story to tell and *Diamonds on the Water* is mine. Although we have largely lost the oral tradition of those who went before us, today we have technology to capture and share the highs, the lows, the lessons, the loves of each life lived. As this season of my life approaches its end, I pray that *'Diamonds'* will inform and instruct, entertain and inspire all those I love." The piece below comprises excerpts from the memoir.

Fishing and Storytelling—gifts of love

I am not sure exactly how tall he was, appearing to my five-year-old eyes to be at least the height of the cane pole he passed to me that morning. Now, fifty years later, my memory of him still seems vague and unfocused. What he has given to me, however, remains as clear today as it was that day, standing next to his shiny black sedan. Grandfather had a great love of fishing and an even greater love of storytelling and that has been his gift to me. I suppose that my purpose in writing this personal recollection is to pass on these stories of fish caught, fish lost and life's lessons learned, to my three sons and their children that they too might feel some of the joy and magic I have experienced on the water. In so doing they might learn a little more about me.

We agreed the night before that as many of us as were up by seven, dressed and breakfasted, would leave the cottage quietly and meet down at Granddaddy's big black car, which was maybe a '48 Buick. Of course, not only was I awake at seven, I was up all night waiting for the moment of departure. It was July 1949, and the cottage was crowded with at least twelve of us, including of course Grandmother and Granddaddy. The cottage was full of activity and this morning we were going perch fishing on the pier.

Somehow, we managed to get all the eight- or ten-foot bamboo poles into the two cars and headed west along Lake Avenue, past the "point," down the hill toward Grand Haven State Park and the pier.

Loch Hame was our cottage and it was to play such an important part in my early life as a fishing disciple. It was the earliest summer home built in what later came to be known as the Highland Park area of Grand Haven. The cottage was built of sturdy 12- and 14-inch boards and batten, had two floors and, much to the delight of generations of McCarthys, Grieves and Reids, had a superb beech tree that grew up through our two porches.

Loch Hame, built in May, 1887, was for a five- or six-year-old, a place of wonderful treasures and fabulous adventure. After driving down the Lake Avenue hill away from the cottage, we turned into the Grand Haven State Park and parked near the minnow shop. This was a fascinating place that smelled heavily of fish and was right on the edge of the river at the start of the pier. As we held out our minnow pails, the men who worked the tanks would take their nets and scoop out silver, slippery minnows by the dozen into our buckets. Some of the minnows were dead or dying.

"Dead minnows are only good for fertilizer," Granddaddy would say. "You need the average size ones, really fresh and lively for the hook."

Once the pails were filled with several dozen perfect minnows, and with the sun at our backs we would begin our long and somewhat treacherous walk out the pier to the ideal spot.

The Grand Haven pier was built as one of many along the coast of Lake Michigan. It was used by the Coast Guard to guide the large lake freighters into the many ports from Chicago in the south to Saginaw in the north. Our pier had both a lighthouse at about the halfway point and a small building at the end that contained the foghorn.

So, we stayed next to the lake and began our walk out to find the perfect spot, Grandfather leading and the rest of us trailing along behind, adults somehow managing to keep kids, minnow pails and poles in tow.

Grandfather would periodically stop and look at the waters closely and then after a moment's thought when we would all try to imagine what issues he was considering, he would have us move on a bit further. Then Granddaddy finally stopped, looked around to see that there was no one too near by and pronounced in his thick Scottish burr that "this was the perfect place for perch and for us."

And so, our day on the water began and my life as a student of fishing and disciple of life's lessons commenced.

Recently I read a quote from Soren Kierkegard that said **"Life is lived forward and learned backward**." Certainly, when

I reflect on my life's lessons this is true. Fishing on the other hand can be learned as one fishes, if one is paying attention.

As the morning drew on, our pail for perch filled, with Granddaddy catching most on his rod with reel, but each of us catching at least a few. By midmorning when the sun was hot and the remaining minnows had rolled over in the bucket, our attention span had diminished and we began the long process of packing up our gear to head home. We were tired, hungry for breakfast and very excited about our fishing adventure.

The biggest catch that day was five-year-old me. I was going to be a fisherman always.

Back at the cottage we turned the pail of perch—there must have been at least forty or fifty—over to Grandmother who happily began one of life's most time-consuming and unappreciated tasks, cleaning our fish.

Granddaddy

John Grieve was born near Edinburgh in Scotland to a wealthy family and, as I understand his story, he was sent to Can-

Below: Peter's Granddaddy and Grandmother

ada to make his way in the new world. On the ship sailing from Great Britain to North America, he made the acquaintance of a young woman and her mother who had been traveling in Europe. The beautiful Isabel McCarthy and the handsome Scot fell in love on board ship and were later married. Grandfather was an engineer, structural I think, and, I believe, spent his early working life building bridges around Canada and the U.S. for Dominion Bridge. My understanding is he may also have worked for a paint company somewhere along the way.

The depression took most if not all of the family fortune, but still the couple produced five healthy children, three boys and two girls and lived quite comfortably.

My earliest memories of Granddaddy are of sitting on his knee, listening to his quiet voice. I would watch him make three-masted schooners out of a single sheet of writing paper or rabbits out of the folded white linen handkerchief he always carried in his pocket. Spellbound, I would listen to his stories of being a young lad growing up in some far-off land. They had lived in a castle or at least in an estate house and to me it was a life full of adventure. He would tell me of the deep well they had on the property that somehow magically had trout at the bottom of it. He would lower his line into the pool at the bottom of the well and sure enough he would soon have his creel, whatever that was, full of shiny silvery trout.

My favourite story was of Granddaddy walking across the hills to his secret brook early in the morning. The dew was still wet on the grass and the sun not yet high enough in the sky to cast long shadows. The stream was not very wide maybe 10 or 12 feet I imagined, but enough breadth to allow small pools to form under the grassy banks as the water meandered its way through the hills, across the glens and around the rocky outcrops of Scotland. A few of these pools and grassy banks were the young John's target. He would slither the last few yards through the wet grass like a snake on the western side opposite the sun, so as not to cast a shadow. When he reached the special pool, he would silently reach over the bank and slide his hand carefully into the cool water. Slowly he would move his hand forward just under the surface until he sensed, as much as felt, the motion of the water in front of his hand.

As I sat on his knee in rapt attention seeing everything in my mind's eye, Granddaddy described how he would gently slide his small hand up under the trout's tail and tickle the trout's underbelly with his middle finger. As he did so, and provided he was very gentle, the trout would lazily slide back into his hand. With one quick motion he would slip his thumb and pointer finger up into the gills of the fish and pick it clean out of the water and toss the wriggling trout onto the bank. These and other similar stories fascinated me and bred my love of the sport.

Retracing Granddaddy's Story

"Of course, it's true! It's even a word in the dictionary, did ya think your grandfather was havin' you on, sir?" With that, Granddaddy left the bar of the Lands of Loyal boutique hotel to find the large dictionary that he promptly opened in front of me and read out the description:

"Guddling—also known as trout tickling was a common practice for catching trout by hand in Scotland and the United Kingdom."

Many years later, I retraced Granddaddy's story on a trip to Scotland. It was a glorious afternoon and I had driven up from Edinburgh to Alyth to stay overnight in my ancestral home; the home of my Granddaddy John Grieve, who had held me on his knee, told me wonderful stories of walking across the fields as a boy and catching trout with his fingers. And now I was in the same home he had grown up in. The magnificent building dominated the countryside of the charming little Scottish town as it peered down over the fields of Perthshire.

I arranged to drive up and spend the night in this beautiful stone building. The weather was spectacular, warm and sunny, as I drove along the narrow, winding roads. As I turned into the long driveway and drove up to the magnificent front entrance, time collapsed for me. I was imagining myself in the late 19th century as a young boy walking over the rolling hills looking for fast flowing burns where I could practice the centuries old poaching art that my Granddaddy described; one that I had over time written off as an old man's fairy tale.

The proprietor had put me up in the master bedroom overlooking the entrance way and now I was trying to soak up as much of the history as I could. I learned that Granddaddy's ancestral home was now called the Lands of Loyal. The 17-bedroom home was built in the 1830's by Sir William Ogilvie, a hero in the Battle of Waterloo. It continued to have a prominent role in the Second World War as it provided refuge to the Polish aristocracy and the extensive gardens were used to support the war effort. One fascinating fact was that the main room and grand staircase were modelled after the infamous luxury liner the *Mauritania* that was used as a troop ship in the North Atlantic.

I sat in the cozy little pub off the main lobby with a glass of decent red wine and the setting sun poured in through the window. Apparently the Grieves were kind of Lords of the Manor in the town of Alyth and I found all sorts of references to them and pictures of what it looked like in Granddaddy's time. I walked to the local church Sunday morning after a full

Below: Peter's ancestral home, Alyth, Scotland

Right:
And back in the 1890's.
(Pic courtesy Alyth HS)

Scottish breakfast that included kippers, blood pudding, toast fingers and boiled eggs. I met a woman who was the head of the Alyth Historical Society and she took me round to the building that housed all the photos and records of the village over the centuries. The photos I took at various points around the village revealed that not much had changed in 120 years compared to the photos of that era.

The village streets, the stone-walled fields of Granddaddy's day were now my own. The stories he shared with me were now my stories to share with my children.

Granddaddy and trains

I remember one summer adventure with Granddaddy that did not involve fishing. I had always had a love for trains for this was the era of the great steam locomotives that carried people and products across the continent from coast to coast. The trains were big, black and powerful. With steam billowing out of the smokestack, boilers consuming great loads of coal, wheels churning. These great beasts were a thing of beauty to me.

As a three- or four-year-old in Toronto, Granddaddy would take me from our home in Forest Hill down to the foot of Bathurst Street or Spadina Road and we would sit for hours watching the great steam trains chug in and out of Union Station. Toronto was the central point for all the passenger and freight traffic headed east to the Maritimes and west to the prairies and beyond. With Granddaddy no doubt showing the patience of Job, I would stay for hours and count the freight cars, describe the coal car, oil cars, caboose, and occasionally get a glimpse of a dome car heading west. The dome car was part of the most beautiful train of all, Canadian Pacific's *The Canadian* powered by not one but several magnificent steam engines on its way west to the Rockies and Vancouver.

I was fascinated by the Round House; that unique pivotal building where the engines would turn around and reposition for another load and another journey. After hours of just sitting and watching all the action on the spider web of track below, Granddaddy would take me up to the Borden's dairy for an ice cream before going home.

Once, Grandmother had to go down to the Grand Haven train station to enquire when the train from St Louis would arrive. Never one to pass up a trip to the lovely old mid-western train station, I went along. I loved the place with its wood benches, big clock and chalk boards announcing departure and arrival times. I was thrilled to find a small shunting engine with a few cars standing in the station alive and breathing. It wasn't long before Grandmother and I convinced the engineer to let us climb on board. Let me be more precise, I convinced Grandmother, who convinced the kind engineer.

A young boy's dream came true. Not only did we get to sit in the engineer's cabin but for the next hour or so I actually got to drive the train (at least I had my hand on the throttle) back and forth from the station to the Spring Lake bridge shunting cars onto sidings and bringing other cars onto different tracks. I discovered there was more to life than fishing.

Loch Hame continued to be our summer destination as the years, then decades went by. Although a few things changed, mostly the town, the beach, sand dunes and the pier remained the same. I fell in love, married Pat and we backpacked around the world for a year. It was 1971 and the only year I didn't go to Loch Hame for the summer. As each of our three sons came into the world we returned to Grand Haven and introduced them to my summer life as a child growing up.

We carved their initials on the beech tree that grew through the porches along side those of their parents, grandparents, great-grandparents, uncles and aunts and countless others they would never meet nor ever know. We sat on the porch and read the Grand Haven Tribune, ate nuts from Fortino's and Bugles from Meijer's, rocked in the same rockers and waited until we were called in for dinner of fresh perch. At night, we told the same stories that generations before had told.

Grandmother, now in her 80's, still came to Loch Hame every summer. She fascinated all of us with stories from her childhood. How her mother had been confronted by an Indian brave who came up on the porch brandishing a knife asking for food. Standing eye to eye, she never backed down and to my memory never gave in to his demand. Or how Levant Rhines, a major in the First Michigan Sharpshooters, was shot dead in the Civil War outside of Petersburg, Virginia, by a Confederate rebel when he stood up in response to the waving Confederate white flag of surrender.

When just a young girl, grandmother and her family had gone west by wagon train out to and through Montana and the wild west. We were riveted as grandmother explained the stories of our American heritage, that our ancestors had arrived on America's shores in Massachusetts on the first ship following the Mayflower. I think that perhaps as we sat there rocking back and forth on the porch rockers that summer at the cottage, I began for the first time to appreciate the value of family history and the need to preserve the stories of our lineage.

We continued to go to Grand Haven every summer until after Gavin, our third son was born in 1980. Our sons learned to choose the right minnows, find the right spots on the pier for perch and walk proudly back with their day's catch.

Eventually grandmother passed away in her early nineties, having lived a full and rich life. Friends with the likes of Aldous Huxley, involved in the establishment of the League of Nations, founder of the Anthroposophical Society in Canada, early founder of Waldorf Schools in Toronto—grandmother was a woman ahead of her time. I was profoundly affected by her life and even more so by her death. In truth, I was so upset by my failure to know her better, I would not attend her funeral; I preferred to remember her rocking gently on the Loch Hame porch, knitting something for a grandchild or sitting in the old cane chair in the living room, reading the Grand Haven Tribune.

Peter's Grandmother

Merridy Cox

Merridy Cox has a B.Sc. in Biology and an M.Msl. in Museum Studies. She has a deep interest in nature and ecology and is often seen outdoors with her camera. She has published poems and her photography in numerous anthologies. She has written two booklets (with photos): *Nature Breaks for Busy Urbanites* and *The Story of Linnaeus and Binomial Nomenclature*. A third book, *A Swan Family's Summer*, with poetry and photos is underway. As an editor, Merridy has worked on several books. She can be reached at LyricalLeafEditing.com.

Adrift

A bird sits fluffed and hunched on the lawn,
waiting for its mother.
Its spotted breast reminds me of a fawn,
curled quietly into a cup of leaves,
taking the scent of the forest—
safe for now.

The oaks reach crookedly for the sky;
the high dappled canopy quivers in the breeze.
A branch creaks.

I sit on the verandah,
wrapped in a spotted shawl,
alone in the corner of a loveseat,
my hands cradling an old photo album.

I watch as daylight diminishes
through lacy sky holes, far above.
Evening flowers scent the air.

Acorns ricochet sharply off
the roof, the stairs, the path—
like bursts of fireworks.

On a branch, a grey squirrel sits,
his tail wrapped over his back,
nose tucked into his chest.

Skywards, the mother robin calls.
Leaves whisper greenly.
The air smells like rain.

Only her photo remains.

Strength of Heart

I was five when my parents bought a cottage in the Near North, in Quebec. For me, an only child, it represented freedom to roam and explore in wilderness. When I was six, a bumblebee caught itself under my hair, and I got a painful sting behind the ear.

At seven, I roamed too far and found myself in a savannah of lichened glacial pavement, jack pine trees and blueberry bushes. No one was in sight. I knew my way home, although it was rather far, but I was as good as lost. The summer air was laden with the scent of pine and wildflowers—and the buzz of bees.

Once I became aware—there were bees everywhere! I felt surrounded.

I stood on the rocks, feeling the crisp, grey lichen beneath my bare feet, searching for the path and seeing only trees and bush—and bees.

If only I could fly, I thought, *I could escape. Why did I come so far, alone?*

A few tears smeared my grubby, sun-kissed face. My voyage of exploration had somehow gone wrong. The first inklings of fear began to seep into my being. The sun began to swing across the sky, but I couldn't move.

Suddenly, emerging from behind some tall rocks and trees, came my Daddy. He enveloped me in a big bear hug! I was rescued. He was as relieved as was I.

"What happened?" he asked.

"I got stuck. I got stuck here because of the bees."

Then, tightly holding Daddy's hand, it seemed the bees didn't matter. We walked home together on the trail hidden in the blueberry bushes, as if nothing could touch us. Mum had dinner waiting for us, after Dad had talked to me a little about what to do when feeling lost.

Since then, I carry some of my father's strength in my heart, and bees have never bothered me again.

Merridy Cox 135

Merridy's parents: Wallace D. (Peter) and Mary Cox

Lillian Khan

Lillian (Sabiha) Khan is originally from India, and now calls Canada her home. Coming from a family of educators, she believes in learning for life. A former marketing consultant, she is currently a licensed payroll compliance practitioner. *Soulfie* (IOWI, 2017) is her first collection of poems in which she presents her journey through life from a soul perspective. For more info on the works of Lillian Khan, visit: soulpoetess.com

Child woman

Too many girls in the land I came from
grew up overnight
into women and mothers
not knowing,
how to value their bodies, spirit and mind.
Losing themselves,
in their men, marriage, work.
Squashing desire and passion.
A survival mindset for some.
Mistress of camouflage.
Becoming invisible,
diminished, overlooked and less than.

Offspring

Mothers and fathers
some already broken
when they come together

Their offspring
like shattered glass
refract reflections
holding the distortion.

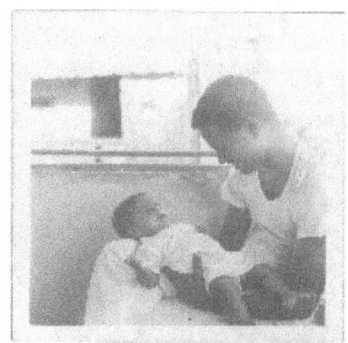

Above: Lillian as a child with her parents
Below: Lillian's parents, Alice and Robert Sequeira

J. Nichole Noël

J. Nichole Noël is a multi-genre writer and performance artist. She has released three audio CDs, eight books of poetry for youth and adults, and several stories for children. Her work has received wide recognition and in 2015, she was listed on Canada's Top 100 Most Powerful Black Women to watch for. She has received numerous awards including the Canadian-Caribbean Award for Best Spoken Word Artist, Community Award for Dub Poetry and ReggaeXclusive Community Award for Reggae Words on Dub. In 2012, she released her CD The Word Heard by Many. In 2004, her first CD, Verse … The Power of the Spoken Word in Music was released in Toronto at the then world-renowned Hummingbird Centre for the Performing Arts. Ms Noël currently lives in Port McNicoll, Ontario, where she runs a bed and breakfast and special events space called Noël's Nest.

Facts of Life According to Mama

One day my Mama decided to sit me down
She wanted to talk about the facts of life
I mean, "The facts of life" according to my Mama

My Mama liked to call herself a realist
When I was a little girl coming of age
She said, "Girl, hold your head high
Don't accept less than the best for yourself."

She said, "When it comes to men …
Between your thighs is the source of your power."
Mama said, "Prepare yourself for lies,
"Lies come in wonderful shapes and colours"
She said, "Find a man who will accept you for who you are"

She then said, "If you find a man that don't treat you good
Reciprocate and treat him like any good woman would
Take him out with the trash on garbage day
And whatever you do … don't bring him back inside
Let the garbage man take him away!"

Dearest Daddy ... Farewell

When I saw your brother, Daddy
I cried twice my size worth in tears
He saw through your eyes, he smiled your smile
He sat straight in his chair and crossed his legs just like you
And I cried twice my size worth in tears

He stood up and embraced my grieving heart
Shattered was my resistance
My clever disguise that I was all right fell to the ground
I could no longer stand strong
I was caught up in childhood memories
My mind replayed joyful childhood stories
Naked in my misery for all to see … me
I cried twice my size worth in tears

Now that you have passed away
Dearest Daddy, hear me this day
Send me some comfort for my bleeding heart
Get better kisses, time won't heal it
Band-aid fixes just won't seal it, only you could find it
 I am lost in the absence of you
Again, I cried twice my size worth in tears

When Uncle Leslie asked me to dance
I upped and selfishly stole the chance
To share one last dance with you
You and I have danced many times through the years
Tonight, upon his shoulders I tattooed my tears
And when your song played, and the singer sang
"As I write this letter, my heart is racing much too fast for my pen,
Soon I will be in your arms again"
At that precious moment in time,

J. Nichole Noel

As Uncle Leslie and I three-stepped across the floor
It was you who were holding me proudly in your arms once more
And I cried twice my size worth in tears

In a room full of well-wishers, I then yearned
Desperately longing for my loved ones back home
Holding tightly onto this emotional ride
Riding the waves in the sea of last good-byes
I await to meet you dearest Daddy, again
My father, my teacher, my fellow poet and friend
Again … I cried twice my size worth in tears

*(Written in loving memory of my father Joseph Dorne Noël
Born July 18th 1933   Died October 6th 2002
Uncle Leslie died September 18th 2003)*

Miranda Wong

Miranda Wong was born in Vietnam and is of Chinese heritage, but has spent most of her life in Mississauga, Ontario, Canada. She works in public service within the legal field. She writes poetry, short stories and lyrics on topics such as equality, discrimination, self-help and mental wellness. She has contributed to e-zines and anthologies.

Parental influence: blessing or curse?

My father's impact on my life is strong and positive, even though he died suddenly at an early age. We were very poor and lived in war-torn Vietnam in the aftermath of Communist rule. We were blessed with a father whose perseverance helped us escape that life. We fled Vietnam with almost 3000 refugees on a freighter called *Skyluck* in 1978, [ed. see YouTube video of ill-fated *Skyluck*]. It is through his heroic actions that we escaped the tyranny of Communist rule and ideology.

Only after my father died, I learned the meaning of my name 'beauty of virtue' and it took me years to understand his gift of my name. He inspired me to live a virtuous life, to choose a righteous path, to care for and do right for others, to respect others and expect respect in return. He taught me to live by example, to manifest self-worth and dignity for my own children.

I learned way more in the short time I had with my father and my observations of his actions. Whenever I was close to rock bottom and was being bullied and assaulted, my dad inspired me to hold on, to believe in myself, to have faith, and to not be swayed by hatred or desire for revenge. His example taught me to become more self-aware and mindful of my own choices and actions. I became philosophical and learned to self-reflect, to discern life lessons from his legacy.

My father's many traits and self-motivating spirit taught me to problem solve, to persevere, and to help me save myself and my children from violent abuse at the hands of my then husband, their own father, who was a narcissist.

Seeing my brother die before his 25th birthday because he could not get a liver transplant, and then losing my father eight years later when I was 24, taught me that we must live today as if it would be our last time together and cherish the relationships and things we are blessed with. I have done my best with what life has bestowed upon me. I followed my father's example and sought help with choosing meaningful names for my own children. Hopefully, my children will be blessed with good qualities in the meaning of their names, and continue this naming tradition.

I learned to openly display affection and communicate my feelings of love—which was so against our traditions.

My mother's impact on my life, on the contrary, was short-term and unhelpful. In the face of constant chaos and overwhelmingly unfair abuse by elders and relatives, her way to survive was to become light-spirited and carefree, and not to worry or look too far ahead into the future. Her perspective has helped her keep her youthful beauty as she aged. She taught me to make easy choices, live in the moment, be more self-serving, and enjoy life as it unfolds.

I generally resemble my father as a worrier and careful planner. However, when things became hopeless for me, I conceded to copy my mother's ways and live life *laissez faire* temporarily for stress release. In doing so, I took up her bad habits of self-indulgence which drove me into debt, clutter and poor health.

In hindsight, my upbringing and difficult circumstances, manifested in the blessed legacy and influence of my father and the instant gratification habits of my mother. The drastic contrast between their traits and perspectives required me to learn self-control, gain perspective and reach a balance in my life.

*Above: Escape from Vietnam on the ill-fated Skyluck 1978
(photo supplied by author)
Below: Miranda's father and parents*

Debra D'Souza-Haroon

Debra D'Souza-Haroon grew up watching many women struggling against oppression, rejection and abuse. Her passion for the empowerment of women through instilling self-worth is demonstrated in her work in Education, both nationally and internationally through various organizations based in Europe. Her mission in life continues through her speaking and writing engagements on various forums.

A seed of hatred

When you left us, a seed of hatred was sown in my heart, which I removed and placed in the palms of God's hands. Your absence came as a blessing in disguise. Growing up with a father who never showed up was like I wore a tag of rejection. You left, showing how unworthy I was to be accepted and capable of being loved. Your name left a stigma on my life. It ruined my sister's life and I learnt valuable lessons in how to resist dejection at another's rejection.

So now, I thank you for not being there in my life, because I had an awesome life without you. Never learnt to rely on a man. You made me a strong girl who grew into an empowered woman and mother. This I learned from my mother.

Falling, tripping and playing with boys never made me afraid, because what I learned, from you, was that men are weak and they run away. The more I lived in your absence, the more it made me independent.

The times I saw my friends with their fathers wiping away their tears, all I knew was I cannot cry because no one will be there to wipe my tears. So, I cultivated joy within me. Thank you for letting me have my joy. Fighting battles, protecting my siblings, for by then I knew we had no superhero father to protect us. You taught me to be the defender that we needed.

As time passed by, your importance almost faded from my life as it was overtaken by the power of my heavenly Father by then. I was safe in the palms of His hands.

Now your chapter in my life story almost became irrelevant because all I knew was that my identity is not defined by your existence or by your absence. So, with an attitude of gratitude, I carry on with my life journey believing and inspiring others to not let their identity be defined by others who fail them. It is you, yourself, that makes you beautiful and unique.

I love you for never showing up.

A Garment of Grace

This is all I remember of my mother. She was graceful as she chose to wear the garment of grace that hid a secret. When she felt empty, she made sure to fill others. Even in her sickness, she was affectionate and giving.

Bearing five kids, who were still minors when she fell ill, deepened her sorrow and she took refuge in silence. The silence weighed heavy on her younger daughter—me—and raised many questions which were left unanswered.

Not long after, her journey ended leaving many unanswered questions and gave rise to much uncertainty. For me, at the age of eight was the beginning of a new journey.

I feel my soul still connected to my mother's, and I have learnt not to be silent, but raise my voice against injustice and deprivation. Against rejection and mistreatment. This is where I decided to fight every battle in life with courage.

My mother taught me in her grace how to be full when you are empty. How to give before receiving. Her unspoken words called out loud to me that a woman is very strong within.

Now I am with my mother in spirit. Life is a battle which needs to be fought. I made sure to do it all from taking risks to making decisions. There was a magical power I felt as if the whole universe opens if I but strive.

I still remember those days when my mom in her last days made sure to hide her pain and give us those final moments of laughter and love. The joy sparkled through her eyes that even today shines through my life.

The rejections she bore with grace worked as triggers in my life and I was determined never to be put down by any sort of rejection, because life is beautiful, and each of us has the right to be happy.

This attitude of gratitude has made me who I am today. A mother of two beautiful daughters and a son. The journey from

Pakistan to Europe was not a piece of cake. Life took a U-turn. Yesterday was hers and today is mine.

So, my mother in her silence taught me to give what I want to receive. My mother gifted me this blessing of grace, which she wore like a garment and I learnt how to wrap myself with it. Whenever I feel broken, she shapes and makes me whole. Her 33 years of absence feels like yesterday as we still hold on to each other through fond memories, which I feel keenly to this day.

Her memory is one of grace.

Below: Debra's mother Mabel D'Souza

Susan Ksiezopolski

Susan Ksiezopolski is an award-winning published author, speaker, coach and facilitator. Her work has been featured in anthologies, magazines and on-line platforms. In 2018, Susan founded WriteWell, supporting organizations and individuals to unleash the creative power of writing, creating a path to success and wellness. A graduate of the Humber School for Writers and a Toronto Writer's Collective Lead Training Facilitator, Susan developed and facilitates creative workshops across the GTA, giving voice to marginalized communities.
Her website is mywordsnow.com

Why

Why was I born
To a mother
That doesn't fit me
Doesn't know how to love me
The way I want to be loved
Why was I born
To a father
That loved me but didn't love
himself enough
And drowned out his own sorrow
slowly snuffing
out his own existence
Why was I born
To a place far away
then transplanted here
Why was I born
To a time
Where change accelerates
Faster than the speed of life
Why was I born
To live a life
Of constant yearning, learning
Why was I born
To be
Who I am
Why was I born
To have
What I have
Why was I born
To know
What I know
What I was born to do

A Daughter's Ode to Dad

Those so many years ago
I just didn't know
That you were the one
Who taught me to be strong
To stand up against wrong
You were the one who saved me
From life's wrath and believed in me
I could be whatever I wanted to be and
Do whatever I wanted to do
And I owe a lot to you

Today I stand
Taking my daughter by the hand
Finally, I understand your pride
Even though at the time I just wanted to hide
Embarrassed by your grandeur words of praise
I now am thankful for those days
I now see them as the winds that set my sails in motion

It was your way to say
"Look at my child and see what she can be"
"Look at my child, she is the best part of my heart"
I'm sorry to have missed the chance
To thank you for the encouragement to stay in the dance
I'm sorry I failed to see
Just how much you were so proud of me
I'm sorry that I didn't get more time
To learn about your life's reason and rhyme
For I think that I would find
That you and I were of similar mind
The conflict that kept us apart
Was in not knowing how to start
To reach and look beyond our minds, inside one another's hearts

So let me say it now in this ode to you

No matter where I go and what I do
My heart will always hold a part of you
You too are one of the best parts of my heart

Below: Susan with her father Ernesto

Lynn Xu

Lynn Xu witnessed the turmoil of Mao's Cultural Revolution, and came to Canada as an adult. Here she began her lifelong journey of learning a new language and a new way of living. She is currently enrolled in a creative writing program at the University of Toronto's School of Continuing Studies. She enjoys writing poetry as a means of 'getting to know' herself and the world.

Remembering Dad

You were named after clouds and passed away around the Full-moon Celebration. Since your passing, each harvest moon reminds me of you. Your absence in form helps me to connect more with you in spirit.

Let me not think of you
as a promise
I broke
nor as a lesson
I failed

But to think of you
as the missing half
that makes the harvest moon brighter
as the floating cloud
that makes the azure sky bluer

Think of you
as my heart's song
expanding and contracting
like an accordion
and then the silence follows
echoing in my mind

Think of you
as part of my own thinking
and part of who I am

Milena Marques-Zachariah

Milena Marques-Zachariah has over 25 years' experience in multinational advertising in India, Dubai and Canada. She is a Creative Consultant and runs her creative shop, OUT OF MY MIND. She has focused on the South Asian and ethnic markets since immigrating to Canada two decades ago. Her sharp insights and thorough knowledge of the multi-cultural markets have led to some ground-breaking advertising in the financial, telecommunications and food industries. This valuable exposure came in handy when she conceived and launched Radio Mango, six years ago—the first and only Konkani language broadcast in North America. She currently writes a blog: *Canadian Chronicles*—inspired by immigrants.

Lessons from My Father

My father did not return the village people's greetings. Not until they addressed him as 'Bhatkar' (landowner in the local language, Konkani) or 'patrao'–(boss in Portuguese). This didn't come from arrogance. He was just a proud man. Proud of his lineage, and where he came from. He was simply a firm believer in hierarchy, and insisted that respect should be given to those who deserved it. Be it landowners, the clergy or even village elders. He respected others, and demanded respect from others.

Papa's personality demanded respect! If you saw a tall, pale-skinned man, walking down the village street, with a hat placed jauntily on his head and a slightly crooked smile—that would be my father: Olympio Salustiao do Rosario Marques. Once the hierarchy was established, and my dad was suitably acknowledged and greeted, everything changed. Then the jokes and teasing began. He spared no one—from the fisherwoman who delivered the freshest pomfret, shrimps, crabs and 'kormot' a medley of the catch of the day, to the barber, who came once a month to give my dad and my brothers a haircut. The baker, who came every morning following the raucous crowing of the rooster, always went away laughing. Papa had something funny to say to everyone. The neighbours' wives were constantly teased, as were the women who helped around the house. Everybody loved his ready sense of humour. The women all blushed at his ridiculous comments, and their husbands were happy to see that my father could get their wives to smile. Papa brought a little sunshine in their otherwise hard lives.

My father spoke English, Portuguese and the local language Konkani, with equal fluency. He wrote with equal ease. His penmanship was something to behold. He took great pride in the very art of writing. The writing was cursive and beautifully crafted. I can still picture the flourish of the pen that seemed to flow and create art on the page. Many relatives and friends have preserved his missives for posterity. He was as meticulous in keeping accounts and wrote everything down in his beautiful writing. Even the smallest purchase was accounted for. That came from his job as a banker. And he always insisted—with little success—that my mother keep accounts. This habit continues with me.

During meals, my father sat at the head of the table, where he presided with some authority. In all my life, I have never seen him use his fingers to eat, which is a typical Goan habit. He always ate with a fork and spoon. I used to marvel at the way he managed to get every morsel of flesh out of bony fish and pick the flesh off meat bones with great dexterity. We kids' often abandoned the cutlery if the fish was difficult to tackle. Not my father! I can still picture him: pink in the face after a hot shower, shirt always buttoned despite the heat, fully focused on eating the delicious meals prepared for him by my mother.

My father was a cool-headed man, rarely provoked to anger. But if the curry was too watery for his taste, or if there was no 'sobremesa' (dessert) he would simply clang the fork and spoon together to display his annoyance. My father had to have his dessert, even if it was a mere banana. No meal was complete, if there wasn't something to sweeten his palate at the end of it. His generosity peaked when we had guests. He insisted on piling food on their plates, always explaining to his horrified kids that most guests were too polite to eat their usual portions and therefore had to be helped. Perhaps, he wasn't entirely wrong.

Papa loved talcum powder which he lavishly dusted himself with, following his daily bath. Ponds Dreamflower Talc. I can recognize that fragrance anywhere, anytime. Because after papa finished, my older brother and I would often rush to do the 'twist' dance in the leftover powder on the floor. What joy! Papa enjoyed this, because he himself was a superb dancer. The waltz, tango and fox trot… it was a pleasure to watch this 6 ft. heavyset man sailing across the room with utter grace, with my 5ft. nothing mama in his arms. For papa, doing things in style was very important. He believed breeding showed through an inherent style money could never buy.

There were many things that were important to him. The quintessential cultural icon of Goa—the 'Konkani tiatr' or theatre had its most loyal patron in my dad. 'Konkani tiatr' was popular for its high entertainment value. Tiatr has always revolved around social, religious and political themes, mirroring the essence of Goan culture. At the time, most educated and upper class Goans didn't patronize tiatrs, but my father always considered this an art form unique to Goa and took us kids along to watch them. His passion for the Konkani language was similar. Again, Konkani as a language was relegated to the kitchens, and rarely spoken in drawing rooms of the Goan gentry. Thanks to the strong belief of my papa, my love for the language grew, which ultimately led me to start RADIO MANGO, the first and only radio in the Konkani language in North America.

And then, at 66, papa suddenly succumbed to a heart attack. One day he was laughing, calling the doctor unmentionable names, and the next day he was gone. Everyone in the village turned up for his funeral. The shopkeepers at the 'tinto' or village square requested my mother to bring the funeral cortege via the Village square, as a tribute to the man who had a kind word for everybody and gave jobs to many in the Village. My papa lives on… in the memories of his six children, and the innumerable lessons we imbibed from him.

I can still picture him… sitting on the easy chair on the 'balcao' or verandah, reading the newspaper, his shiny, bald pate visible from a mile away. Passers-by always stopped to have a laugh with him or enjoy a little teasing.

But first, they all knew they had to wish him in a proper manner.

Milena's parents on their wedding day

Lovina D'Souza

Lovina D'Souza is a photographer and writer. Originally from India, she loves travelling and seeing the world through her 'special lens.' Her hobby of photography turned into a business 'Photographer La Vie' with encouragement from family and friends. Lovina spends much of her leisure time volunteering in her community. photographerlavi.wixsite.com/lavi

A Blessing in our Lives

My Mom turned 93 on November 3, 2019, and I reflected on how very blessed and fortunate I am to be her daughter. I am so proud to be able to write this tribute to her about her influence in my life.

Emilda Mary Rodricks (my Mom) was born in Puttur, Karnataka State, India. She migrated to Toronto, Canada, and has adapted very well in this country.

She is such a strong influence on me and my entire family. Her positive attitude and joy for life fills our home with love.

My Mom is always active and stays busy. She is a keen gardener and grows vegetables and flowers...from digging to seedlings to harvesting, even to this date when she is 93.

Mom is very fond of singing and has an above average memory. She can recite Shakespeare which she studied in Grade 10 and remembers poems that she helped my brother memorize when he was in school. She knows the Latin prayers by heart, which she helped her own brother memorize as an altar server trainee in church, back in the old days.

Mom loves reading and is up to date on the news and talk show discussions.

I pray that God may continue to keep my Mom in good health and happiness always and grant her a long life.

Lovina's Mom:
Emilda Mary Rodricks

Jasmine Jackman

Jasmine Jackman is a Vice Principal and equity and social justice advocate. She is passionate about teaching culturally responsive and relevant pedagogy, volunteering, and working with youth in underserved communities. She has served extensively on the boards of non-profit organizations. She is currently pursuing her PhD in Educational Leadership and Policy at the Ontario Institution for Studies in Education at the University of Toronto.

Dear Daddy

excerpts from a letter to my father

I remember
standing on your feet, as a child,
and hugging your knees
as you walked around
How you plopped us around your shoulders
when we were too tired to walk

enveloped us in a great big hug
when we sobbed uncontrollably
rocked us to sleep in the crook of your arm
that was always the best medicine

when we got lost in a crowd
all we had to do was look up
and we could see you
towering head and shoulders over all
our friendly giant

I always wondered if you found it impossible
to show weakness
perhaps you wanted us
to have someone strong to look up to?
Then one day as you stood by the graveside
of your cousin, holding my hand
I looked up and there were tears awash
I knew then even daddies cry

I remember coming home late from work
one winter's night
And four blocks short of home—a blizzard struck
the buses were late or put out of service

I stood by the roadside, no shelter from the cold
No hat or gloves in the frigid air
I called for you to pick me up
I could barely feel my feet
Your car would not start
so you came on foot
carried me home, cloaked under your coat

I remember when my obstinacy ruled
when I left studies and went off to Europe
You shut me out—silent for that entire year
Though we disagree
I know your love is always there

And when I brought my first boyfriend home
you were surprisingly civil
even though he rode a motorcycle
When some short months later he asked for my hand
I could see the pride in your face
but also a tinge of sadness

On my wedding day as you walked me down the aisle
I saw you hesitate and a tear welled up in your eye when the priest
asked you who gives this woman to this man
You cleared your throat said I do and took your seat next to mom

Now the years have past by and your health has declined
A wicked sign of old age as you move from independence to
dependence
Although our roles are changing
and I assume the role of the parent
know this: I am here by choice not obligation
for love, not duty

I hope you remember, daddy,
how much I truly love you.

My Mom

A lifetime of memories, Mom
of lessons, of love
you bequeathed your kids

I am writing them down
as kids' stories
for your grandkids
and great-grandkids
and on and on

So the very best of you
will live on forever.

Love you, Mom

Jasmine's parents: Father in white jacket; mother, seated left

P.I. Kapllani

Përparim Kapllani (**P.I.Kapllani**) was born in the city of Elbasan, Albania. He came to Canada in 2000, bringing with him many untold stories. He graduated as Anti-Aircraft Gun Artillery Officer in 1990. Eight years later, he graduated as a high school teacher for Literature and Albanian Language from the University of Tirana. A prolific author, Perparim has published numerous books in Albanian and in English, the most recent being *The Thin Line*, Mawenzi House, 2018. He has published extensively in Canadian anthologies and his novella *The Hunter* was shortlisted by Quattro Books for The Ken Klonsky novella contest in 2015. He was a journalist with *Ushtria*, the Albanian Army Newspaper and *Shekulli* and other daily Albanian publications.

The Madman

(A chapter from Particles—*a novel by P.I. Kapllani)*

"Don't look at the madman!" she whispered. *"Don't turn your head!"* Mother squeezed his hand tightly and forced him down the street and urged him not to look at the other side of the road.

The Fish Palace received its strange name from a fish shop located on the first floor of the building. The Palace had originally served as a bachelor's hotel.

If you ran your hand over the bricks of the two-story building, the mortar crumbled under your fingertips. Above the fish shop, the Palace housed eighteen families living in twenty-five rooms, privacy was maintained by thin reed walls. Neighbours' snoring and almost all conversations were easily heard. Kerosene burners were seen along the corridor beside many doors. When they were turned off after cooking, the smell of kerosene exhaust was bad enough to make you feel ill.

The seven public bathrooms were built in the courtyard of the Palace. In most cases, the bathrooms were clogged and the smell of feces wafted up the main staircase. The swarm of flies wreaked havoc, though residents tried to keep the washrooms clean, washing and disinfecting them whenever they could.

There was only one tap in this Dantesque building, in front of which women and children lined up with buckets and plastic containers. The women were seen washing clothes and hanging them on wires in front of windows, and also in the yard, along the side wall of the building. There was a warehouse on the first floor, which was rat-infested.

The main gate to the courtyard was only a few meters from Thoma Kalefi Elementary School. The yard buzzed with the cheerful voices of the students. As soon as the final bell rang, Nertila, the teacher signaled to Redon to stay after class. The 10-year-old black-haired little boy wondered what mistake he had made that his teacher would keep him after class.

"Redon, is your mom at home?" she asked in a soft voice.

"Yes, she's at home!" He answered.

"Tell her that we're coming to visit you. Happy birthday, Redon!"

That morning his mother had given him a full bag of candies, which he gave away as soon as he entered the class that morning. Still he was surprised that the teacher wanted to visit their home. Their one-bedroom apartment was very small for a family of four.

Redon raced home. "Mom! Mrs. Nertila is here!"

He was worried his mother would not have time to clean up before the visitors arrived. But his mother smiled at Redon, rubbed her hands briskly against her apron. Redon looked up to see the single room arranged like never before. Everything was gleaming with cleanliness, with a bunch of flowers on the dinner table. There were four wooden chairs around, put out only when visitors were expected. Perhaps mother was aware of the visit of the school teachers. She let out a laugh as she watched Redon's face relax into relief.

"Let them come," she said briefly and opened the door. Redon wasn't a shy guy, but that day he was worried. What if a mouse appeared while the teachers were still there? Oh, there would be no greater shame. Although Hamdi had set mice traps

Below: The Fish Palace

around everywhere, the rodent problem had only increased. To dispel the last of his fear at the visit he ran all the way down the corridor where there was a large window with broken glass looking out over the school. He saw the teachers walking over, talking to each other. Teachers Vilma and Nertila were on their way. He felt overcome and returned to the one-room apartment where his mother was waiting.

"Mom, they are here!" he said nervously. Manushaqe hurried before her son to the main stairs of the Palace. The teachers, paused at the door. Though they had been in the place before they always entered with an awareness of the squalor of the Palace. Vilma gave Redon a book of Migjeni's poems (a famous Albanian poet), bound with a red ribbon.

"This gift is for you," Vilma. That special book immediately caught his attention. He held it reverently.

His mother Manushaqe and the teachers spoke in low voices, trying not to let Redon hear them.

"How did you end up like this?" asked Vilma, with wide eyes. She spoke carefully so as not to hurt Manushaqe's pride in her home. It was obvious the place had been tidied up for their arrival and yet it still looked run-down. Manushaqe was comforted, she wanted to tell her story and trusted these women with it.

Manushaqe related how her ex-husband Isa had in a fit of mad rage attacked her with a knife. She had been forced to jump off the balcony to the floor below, hurting her knee, but still she ran on to the police station.

"When I saw the frightened faces of my two little angels, I knew I could not be a coward. Someone had to take care of those kids. I made a report at the police station and they kept me from returning home until they could investigate. They sent Isa straight to the hospital, and the two kids joined me. There was no greater joy when I realized that Isa had not even touched a hair on their heads. We stayed with my first cousin for a few days, while sending the children to Berat city, where my people lived.

"A few months passed and my three brothers asked me to marry again, or go back to my parents' house. So, I married

Hamdi and brought the boys here. When we chose this place, we were told it would be renovated shortly. It's been three years, but no change. As the time passes things feel worse." Manushaqe's eyes shone with tears. Her thin hands trembled. Vilma took them gently in her hands and caressed them.

"How can bright young Redon learn here? You have no place to even breathe," Vilma spoke softly.

"Look, it's not so bad," sighed Manushaqe.

"Why not let Redon use our classroom to study."

Manushaqe didn't know what to say. Her voice cracked as she expressed gratitude to the women who cared for her son.

"May God bestow upon you only joys and happiness in your families," Manushaqe cried out. "I'm so sorry that I bothered you with my life story!"

"Don't worry," Vilma smiled. "We are always here for your family, you can come to us to discuss anything you wish."

"Let it be in the past! You have two boys who are bright as lights, you have to think of them now."

The teachers left the apartment, leaving a sense of security and hope behind. Manushaqe followed them to the courtyard, where they continued their conversation as lively as before. Redon looked out at the large courtyard gate and tried to decipher his mother's gestures. Somehow he knew the conversation was about him. His mother returned quickly.

"When was the last time you met the madman?" She asked suddenly, not looking her son in the eye as she usually did.

"I do not know! Maybe six months ago..." Redon couldn't remember exactly the day he last saw his father. He knew his dad had been hospitalized and often wondered about him.

"Your aunt Nirvana will visit him on Sunday. It's good for you and Plato to go there with her!" Manushaqe's face reddened. She always looked ill when someone mentioned her ex-husband.

Particles of memory came back to him. *When he was on the boulevard with his mother, on the other side of the street he saw his father. Oh, how he had wished that his mother would lift her head and greet his father, who so impatiently waited on the other side of the road, but in vain.*

"Don't look at the madman!" she whispered. "Don't turn your head!" Mother squeezed his hand tightly and forced him to continue down the street and not look at the other side of the road. Panicking, his mother seemed to rush to get the hell out of there.

"Who will take us to the hospital?"

"Aunt Nirvana will come Sunday morning and pick you up. He had come and met the teachers! Nirvana is such a witch!" Mother sighed deeply, as if to remove some of the anger towards her former sister-in-law. "Sweetheart! I want you to be a good student in school. I'm so proud of you!"

Manushaqe was not happy about the two boys meeting Nirvana. The ex-sister-in-law did not forgive Manushaqe for separating from her brother Isa and blamed her for the divorce. Manushaqe wanted to erase any memory of the past. She wanted to break off any contact with anyone who brought back those sad memories.

This time there were teachers involved and there was nothing she could do to stop it. Brokenhearted, she finally agreed to let the two boys meet their father.

Perparim with his father Isa and grandfather

Cheryl Antao-Xavier

Cheryl Antao-Xavier writes poetry, fiction and non-fiction. She has published four books, two collections of poetry; a kids' book series entitled *Life in Maple Woods*; and a self-publishing guide series. But her great passion is mentoring authors through the publishing process. thepublishingmentor.com

Going Home

For my mother, Bertha Fernandes-Antao

What would you do if we come home?
Will you be by the garden wall
peering past the bougainvillea
watching for the first sight of us?
And when you see us coming,
will you hurry indoors
to put the kettle on
for a nice cup of tea?
Will you get busy making vermicelli,
suji halwa or everyone's favourite
green dal with coconut and Goa jaggery?
Or slice open freshly-delivered *karak* rotis
and smother each half with a pat of butter,
homemade mulberry jam
and a dollop of thick cream,
skimmed off home-pasteurized milk?

If we knew you were waiting,
we would leave everything
and come home.

Paradigm shift

Will I forever be watching for
clouds to darken my horizons
and miss the flowers at my feet
picked by small, loving hands?

Innocent eyes watch me
tiny feet shuffle in my footsteps.
My every mood caught and mirrored
with frightening clarity
forcing me
to forget the cautions
of monsoons past
and splash in puddles
welcome the cleansing rain
and keep an eye out for rainbows.

Parenting Revised

He walks out the door,
18 years of over-confidence belied
in the nonchalance of his slouch.

I question or pry, he says,
where are you off to?
Who with?
Do you know what curfew means?

Seeking to forestall mishaps,
getting nowhere close to the attention
my mother received
when instilling the fear of God and man,
sending her daughters off into life,
quiet, reserved, cautious.
She forewarned of vices that stalk virtue.
It was her way of looking out for us.

Not wanting to hold him back,
I revise parenting.

He walks out the door,
teenage eagerness ready to experiment
with vice and virtue
to decide for himself wrong and right.
My heart follows him with a blessing.

Bangles

Gold bangles softly clinked
As she needed flour for chappatis
Tinkled like windchimes
As she scrubbed our clothes
And spun her sewing wheel
Moving those ever-busy hands.
They jingled a warning
When she wagged a reproving finger
To check our wayward ways.
The years of our youth
Were filled with the music of clinking bangles
Blending with our maturing sense of love,
Of home and of motherhood.

And the music of bangles
lives within me.

I pray it never stills,
For I love the sound of tinkling bangles.

With us always

(for my father, Stanley Francis Antao)

His picture held pride of place
in our living room
keeping his memory alive.
We never forgot
or were allowed to forget
all those years,
all those miles away,
that the roof over our heads
the food on our table
the money in the bank
were there because of him.
And so, we grew
from rebellious youth
to young women
to middle age
conscious of his memory.
It is as if he lives
right here in our homes
in Canada and in Australia
where he never set foot
in all his life.
Yet we see glimpses of him
in the mirror
in the eyes of our kids
in the shape of their faces
in the quick temper
and the wide smile.

He never left us.
We never left him.